1965

ık may be kept

But What Is Greatness

Mother Mary Odilia

But What Is Greatness

AN ACCOUNT OF THE LIFE OF

MOTHER MARY ODILIA

Foundress of the Sisters of St. Mary

by SISTER MARY GABRIEL, SSM *and* JANE L. BERDES

SISTERS OF ST. MARY

St. Louis   1959   *Missouri*

DECLARATION

In conformity with the Decree of Pope Urban VIII the authors of this narrative do not intend in any way to anticipate the judgment of the Holy See, to which they submit unreservedly.

NIHIL OBSTAT:

Rt. Rev. William M. Drumm, censor librorum
Sti. Ludovici, die 15 mensis Octobris, 1959

IMPRIMATUR:

✝ Joseph E. Ritter
Archiepiscopus Sti. Ludovici
Sti. Ludovici, die 15 mensis Octobris, 1959

Library of Congress Catalogue Number: 59-15707

MANUFACTURED IN THE UNITED STATES OF AMERICA

BY THE MARQUETTE UNIVERSITY PRESS, MILWAUKEE, WISCONSIN

Contents

Foreword

This is the story of Mother Mary Odilia, the Foundress of the Sisters of St. Mary of the Third Order of St. Francis. Like all true biography it contains not only the events of her passing years but a portrait of her character and the spiritual motivations which gave being to her life work.

By Divine Providence this work in the Institute she formed extends beyond her own life time and it will continue as long as there are Sisters of St. Mary. In this splendid Community, the happy fruit of her aspirations, we see reflected faithfully the great spiritual personality of Mother Mary Odilia herself.

By the same token the traits of soul revealed to us in these pages explain the progress made by her Daughters to the present time. There characteristics, which are the inheritance of the Sisters of St. Mary, prompt us to congratulate them on the larger future in store for them in assuaging the ills of suffering humanity in the name of Christ, Our Lord, and His Blessed Mother.

✠ Joseph E. Ritter
Archbishop of St. Louis

St. Louis, Missouri
October, 1959

Preface

We LIVE IN A world that is exclusively material in an age when success is pursued to a high degree. The worldly success struggle, whether it is for wealth, fame, power, or, as is often the case, for all three, mirrors the spiritual success struggle in which the soul seeks another kind of Trinity—the Father, Son, and Holy Spirit. While the struggles are broadly synonymous, they are even more paradoxical. We see repeatedly in lives of saints that God's formula for success counters that of the world, for His leads away from the world and is rarely appreciated by those who live merely in man's world.

Catherine Berger, a native of Bavaria, foundress of the nursing order of Sisters of St. Mary of the Third Order Regular of St. Francis in St. Louis, employed herself in God's business, the sanctification of souls, by living in man's world and ministering to suffering bodies. She was called upon to give continuously throughout her life. Although poor to the point of having nothing but herself to give, she gave completely knowing that she was but an instrument of God Who has all things to give to His creatures.

Mother Mary Odilia, the name Catherine bore as head of a religious community, was nearly fifty years old when she disembarked in America to toil in the soil of service to others. It seems providential that her roots which lie deep in a land that today is imprisoned behind the Iron Curtain have born fruit apace with the ever developing American Midwest. Her life in the old country had been marked mostly by poverty, sorrow, and repeated failure.

Mother was a serene soul, nevertheless, for all her actions were in obedience to the magnetic command that so moved our holy patron, St. Francis of Assisi, "Provide neither gold, nor silver, nor brass in your purse, nor scrip for your journey."

The temper of her life changed little despite the transplanting, yet today the flowering of the life work of our pioneering foundress is evident in the thirteen splendid hospitals that spread her boundless charity throughout the country. Just as the hospitals and the prospering religious community she established are monuments testifying to the greatness of our humble Mother, so her soul is a monument testifying to the infinite perfection of God's grace and love for His humble creatures.

Pope Pius XII in a diamond jubilee message to us all reiterated the call that embodies the life and love of our Mother:

> And where will you find Jesus if not in His members? If you love the Christ, if you would serve the Christ, love His members, serve His members. Your vocation calls you to serve His suffering members and those too easily, perhaps, neglected by a thoughtless, impatient, self-seeking world.

In the way that Mother Mary Odilia relied wholly on the Divine Will of her Spouse for her inspiration, the Sisters of St. Mary have turned to her as their "Inspirator." Her example has actively impressed three generations of women who continue her work of charity. We know we are seeing as if in a mirror. We credit the remarkable advance of the work of the order in its eighty-seven years of existence to her harvest. In tribute nearly 600 Sisters of St. Mary, all her children, hail her, their spiritual Mother, as a Valiant Woman "whose many daughters gather together to call her blessed."

CHAPTER ONE

Who Shall Find a Valiant Woman?

F RAU BERGER heard the midwife mutter, "Everything is all right, praise God." She knew at last that the most frightening yet the one magnificent experience of her simple life was ended. Mutely, she watched the activity that revolved around her, allowing the fact that she had just given birth to twin daughters to sink into her brain.

In the upper story of the rustic inn, beneath its peaked roof and surrounded by sunrays streaking through the leaded oriel windows of her family's private apartment, she knew that just as her big task was finished, so was the day. Even the twilight would soon be gone due to the rapid sinking of the vivid sun behind the ubiquitous Alpine hills. Close-by, she watched shadows playing impishly on the broad-beamed ceiling, on the somber crucifix hanging opposite her, on the hulking highboy cluttered with unfamiliar paraphernalia of the day's event, on the three neighbor women, weary but *sympathisch* both in words and in action. From below came the growing rumble of feet and chairs and conversation. The workers were gathering for *dunkle*.

"*Ach,* so tiny but so much noise," said the midwife jovially. The women helping chuckled as they dried the newborn infants and cuddled them in warmed flannel. The birth of twins in the cozy Southern Bavarian village of Regen, was truly an occasion on this thirtieth day of April in 1823. The three of them shared a common pride in being part of Katerina Berger's triumph as well as her first delivery.

"It's time for Herr Berger to come," the woman in charge advised gently. They all were preparing to leave. The young mother reached yearningly for the new life, new lives, she reminded herself, so red, so adorable. Each infant was placed aside of her, and she pressed it tightly to her with a rush of love. She smiled tenderly from one to the other before her gaze rested on her bewildered husband, just entering. Herr Berger shuffled to where she lay holding his own two babes in the great feather-bundled bed.

"*Grüss Gott,*" he mumbled as he searched for words to express the riotous feeling inside his whole body that he did not understand. "Oh, *mein* Katie, thank you, thank you." He pressed his hands as gently as he knew how to her wan cheeks. "*Wie geht's?*"

His wife smiled sweetly. "God has blessed us in a great way, Hans," she reassured him. "Don't be worried. Do you like your babies?" Herr Berger nodded, his gray eyes popping and his yellowing teeth all visible in the enthusiastic grin that turned his cheeks into plump prunes. He straightened up and sopped the wetness from his forehead and hair with his apron. The ordeal had turned him into a tired man.

"What names shall we give to our little girls, my husband?" she mused thoughtfully. "You know today is St. Catherine's holyday."

"*Ya,* and Catherine is your name, too, Katie. Which baby came first? She shall have the double honor. And . . . my mother was called Caroline. That sounds good with Catherine. If it is agreeable to their fine mother, the twin girls will be Catherine and Carolyn Berger. What say you?" The matter of names was settled and would be made permanent in a solemn baptismal ritual soon to come.

The climax of a long day's work and a long day's wait had come and gone for the Bergers. Frau was spent. She lay back heavily on the soft pile and hardly knew the sleeping infants were lifted from her arms. A relief like she had never known was overpowering her and she did not want to resist, "It's over. Finished, dear Lord," she whispered the words over and over at first to her husband, then silently to herself. She slept deeply, peacefully.

Herr Berger looked at her understandingly. The deep brown eyes from which he drew so much strength were covered with lids stretched thin. The brow was a little lined, the skin a little coarse, the bloom in her prominent cheeks gone. It did not matter. This woman who had borne him children. His wife. She taught him what it was to love. He would not undervalue her, nor his daughters, nor his happiness.

Hans' thick nailed shoes bulged as he thumped down the worn oak stairs. The mystery of time, of life, of death absorbed his thoughts. Impatient men clear across the long room glanced up full of curiosity at the innkeeper's coming. They saw his perspiration-drenched gray *joppe,* swaying to his still youthful step, his fleshy lips pressed into a long smiling line, eager to blurt out his news as he approached his friends.

"Ah, *ya,* Hans! Tell us the news!" one of them called out familiarly.

The face of Herr Berger broke into a reflection of joy. "My friends, uh, my wife, *mein* Katy, she . . . the baby has come. It's . . . it's two."

"Twins?" The group repeated with amazement and lifted their mugs of dark beer in a common greeting. *"Prosit!"*

Among the dozen tables around which gathered clusters of workmen were new and old friends of the innkeeper, young and old, some who had come to the Berger Inn for food and drink and good times since the days when the senior Herr Berger was its host, and Hans, only a helper.

"*Ya,* twins," he repeated, full of good humor." "Two of them."

"They are boys, Herr Berger?" questioned dour old Jacob, the sheepherder, twisting his inky mustache.

"No, no, my babies are females," returned the new father frankly. In his heart Herr Berger understood the unspoken meaning in old Jacob's voice. Though he had often asked himself what he *would* do if daughters came to him instead of sons, now — in reality — he was calm in the face of it. Such provincialism was

3

almost sacrilegious now that he had seen the vision of new life upstairs.

Persistently, the old man plopped the half-filled mug down on the thick table with diffidence. Moving closer to the big man, he hunched his already stooped back and grasped the innkeeper's dangling arm. He meant to assuage the wound he believed he had delivered to Hans. "We're sorry, Herr Berger. Too bad they aren't boys. Boys would be so much better to help you in your business."

Hans Berger was at first stunned by the awkward reception of his glad tidings. Taking in breath enough as if to blow out the nipping flame of heresy, he bellowed, *"Ach, der lieber."* His chest stretched with pride. "Why should I complain?" he asked to no one in particular. "It's two I got, not one. Without even asking. And the girls are good ones too. Look at my Katy upstairs. A harder working woman I never saw. She gives me two children at one try. They are our children. Or maybe it is better that I should say God's children. Anyway, someday, you will see—I too will have sons to fill your steins," he laughed at them in friendly triumph.

"Come, everybody," he called to the men in the room. "I am happy. But what is the use of trying to be happy at all unless you are happy with somebody?" Herr Berger threw open the doors to his heart and his house in the true spirit of *gemutlichkeit* which is the hallmark of Bavarian hospitality.

He ordered brought out the round, yellow cheeses and he cut them in thick hunks. The celebrated Bavarian beer flowed freely. *Schweinshaxe,* sausages, sauerkraut, pretzels were abundant. There was gay, thigh-slapping music and dancing — all for the welcome of a pair of helpless, unknowing babes still unaware of the life that was theirs.

CHAPTER TWO

She Will Render Good

CATHERINE BERGER and her sister Caroline were born into a land famed for its malt, coal, and salt industries. Bavaria, a German independent state the size of all of Austria, in the very beginning was blessed with the beauty of mountains. It is a perfectly blended conglomeration of all the virtues of nature-rolling plains, always green and golden, a tonsure of spiralling pine and spruce, a crown with snow covered points.

The twin girls were born into a people equally secure and genuine, full of comaraderie and the joy of living, yet sober and moral. Where a German is known for his fortitude and determination, a Bavarian is easy going, independent. Catherine and Caroline knew Bavaria as a country shut out from the exterior world by the Alps, as one that scarcely anyone ever left because it was so easy to be happy there.

They were born into a time when Bavaria was under the rule of the Wittlesbach family. Catherine and Caroline were two years old when the great Ludwig I began the reign of modernizing Bavaria which continued until 1848, their twenty-fifth years. They were born into the tiny Regen village on the important Regen river deep in the Bavarian forest, near Deggendorf. A few hundred villagers who carried on traditional Regen trades of creating organs, precision instruments, beer, and matches also lived in Regen. The picturesque Staudpfarkerche dominated Regen. The old church built in the eleventh century and situated as it still is on the high

5

Pfahl, affords one of the finest views of the entire Bavarian forest and the Regen valley below.

Regen was the world to the little girls whose play-filled days were spent in scampering through the woods and in conquering new adventures among the ruins of the ancient fortress of the Wiessenstein castle. They whispered in awe at the medieval images evoked in the old drawbridge, towers, and crumbling *donjon*. The building that was their particular favorite was the church. Second-best ranked the gathering place of Regen villagers, the Inn, their home.

The Berger twins were born into a home of three rooms of their father's *gasthaus* and around the corner from a vague parade of faces: faces of those people with whom they learned to share their home, the inn, their table, and even their adored parents. The Berger Inn was the center of village activity, perhaps because their inn was a convenient gathering place, perhaps because of its homey, sincere hospitality. From it emanated a wealth of good fellowship and most of the social events of Regen.

This salty summer afternoon in 1837, Katerina Berger sat on a low stool in her open kitchen bending over cherries and cherry stones. She was an understanding, pleasant-looking woman now, aging, whose hair was no more all black and shiny. It was canning time, and Frau Berger was proud both of the quality of her products and of the plenty in her pantry. She sat as she worked for she was weary from the earlier chores. Already that day she had prepared many breakfasts and scrubbed the dishes, had blessed many beds with fresh linen, had polished the tavern floor. Above all, she had cared for her family, now six in number. She had fed, washed, dressed, even sewn a little, for her two younger daughters: Maria, who was nearly six and ready to start school at the twins' Ursuline academy, and Johanna, a toddling three year old.

"Four daughters," she smiled at her work. "Little ones, big ones. The little ones keep me busy and laughing. The big ones help me so that I am not really so busy, yet they stop my laughing with all their problems and goodness." She shook her head slowly.

Frau Berger's day began at dawn every day and seldom stopped before midnight. She knew she had a generous supply of

6

energy and strength by nature, so the work was not a burden to her.
In fact, she would not have been the happy woman she was if she
could not have spent that supply. She was a simple woman who
tried to be pleased with whatever life gave her. Everything she did
for the children, for their home, for her Hans, for the public Inn
was done with love. She felt strongly that of all the others her job
as mother of these four daughters was the most special one. True,
she felt pride in sharing her husband's tasks. The inn was full time
work for both of them. They were busy enough so as not to deceive
themselves that life was anything else but a struggle. But her
daughters. She had great dreams for them, nevertheless. The pig-
tailed *kinder* pushing now at the big bowl nestled in her abundant
lap, all smeared red with the fruit, well, their dreams were not so
clear. But for Catherine and Caroline, her fine fourteen year old
twins, that was a different matter.

"Caroline is our saint. The way she runs up the hill to spend
her afternoons in the *kirche* and talking to the good sisters at school
so that she comes home late for supper. She will make a good nun.
That is what she has always wanted. The way is clear for her. She
must have all the education she can get so she can be a good teacher
someday. Maybe she will teach her own little sisters at the academy.
Too bad really that the four of them are not closer. Caroline has no
time for the babies. . . . *Ach, kinder,* scoot, run out and play in the
court yard now. Run.

"But at least she and Catherine have always had each other,
and the babies are together. It is not so bad. And how will Catherine, dear Catherine, come?

"She says she too wants to take herself to a convent, but she
is always here to help me, to play with the little ones, to take over
for Hans with the serving. She is a homebody, I am almost sure
of it. I was just like her when I was her age. It would hurt me
terribly to let her go away. We are so close. She is really my
strength, though I am sure the idea has never entered her selfless
head.

"Besides I want her to know the wonderful joys of the world,
the good, holy joys. She likes people so much — and everyone is
so drawn to her — she is just not meant to go to the convent. She

is cut out to be a *hausfrau* here, to be a happy mother . . . and a wife . . . like me. *Ach,* when I was her age I had notions about the convent just like her, until I met Hans . . ."

Catherine, tanned and sturdy-looking, came to the doorway carrying a basket of clothes from the fresh air. She set the load down carefully and stood watching the stout figure whose thick back and shoulders bent but did not move as she worked. She did not see her dear mother as a seer trying to divine her children's futures, but only as a mature friend who was wrinkling her cheeks and eyes with a secret smile. "How is the jam coming?" she asked good-naturedly going for a look into the brass kettle.

"Oh, Katy, I've been waiting for you to come," answered the *frau* eagerly. "I am nowhere near finished and someone must get to poor old Jacob Gottlieb's with some food and medicine. Poor man. He's sinking."

"Ya, *mutti.* Can I finish the cherries for you, so. . . ."

"*Nein,* I would rather you go there for me today. My legs are tired. I'll keep with this, and you put the lid tightly on the little soup pot and carry it with you. You'll have to put a fresh cloth on his leg sores, but you've watched me do it enough, haven't you? And the ointments, be sure to take everything you'll need."

She did as her mother advised. Just as she was wrapping up the bandages Caroline who was darker and slimmer came into the room. "Where to, Catherine?" She agreed to go too with Catherine. The gay, young laughter of the girls as they left the Inn made *Frau* Berger exclaim to herself, "I hope I am not doing wrong by exposing the pretty things to all the sadness of sickness and poverty too early."

It was a tiring climb uphill to Herr Gottlieb's cottage. The girls exchanged many greetings with the townsfolk along the way. They had come this way and many other ways often with their mother as she came with help for people she had heard were in need. They shared a deep admiration for their mother from always seeing her be so kind. Catherine especially had watched the gratitude pour out from the eyes of the poor people who her mother cared for and tried to understand how they felt.

They walked carefully, their colorful *dirndls* swinging on the dusty path in rhythm to their steps. They wore square-necked muslin blouses with widely puffed sleeves over their skirts and gaily ornamented vests of the same deep red shade. Three rows of braid hid the hemline. Each girl had a wide, full mouth and broad nose, large wide-set eyes of light brown under dark, protective brows. Their foreheads were spacious. Over all was thick brown hair plainly done in winding braids after a center part. The girls were large boned but short and from them emanated an unaffected sweetness.

In Caroline all this was underplayed; in Catherine it was emphasized.

They were arm in arm, their packages constantly being reshuffled. As they crossed the foot bridge over *Steinerne Brucke,* Caroline broke a thoughtful silence that had been between them, "It's good to help people, isn't it, Catherine?" Her sister nodded without speaking. "How I do admire you and mother the way you like to get into the dirt and squalor and clean the people up and all. I just wonder how you can stand it?"

"I never really thought about it that way," began Catherine. "I just know it is good to help people because they need help so much, and if we don't help them, nobody does. It seems to me that even though we are pretty poor at home, we are rich in many ways. And God would want us to share what we have with people who need something we have."

Suddenly Caroline exclaimed, "Oh, dear, how I want to be a nun! I want to make sacrifices too, I always have. But I want to be something different than Ursuline like we have at school. Do you think I'm crazy, Katy?"

"Hardly," her twin said in reply. Then Catherine spoke in a voice so firm it frightened Caroline. "I want to be a sister in the convent, too, when I grow up. It's all I want. I want to spend all my time taking care of people and making them happy — like the way *mutti* does. And I will too."

Caroline waited a moment, then asked her sister, "Maybe we could stay together even when we are nuns, Katy." And her sister quietly repeated, "Maybe."

9

Arriving at the sick man's house, they knocked and entered the open doorway. Inside they saw a withered body on a cot placed conspicuously in the center of a close, cluttered room. *"Guten Abend,* Herr Gottlieb," said the girls merrily, not looking around the room but rather going to the old man. Catherine bent down to talk to him and spoke loudly to make sure he could hear. "How are you today, sir? And are the legs feeling better?" Defty, she unwrapped the cloth and caught the oozing liquid in it. "Why don't you sweep up a bit and warm the soup, Caroline?" she suggested, realizing that her twin sister should not watch. She busied herself making the miserable old one clean and more comfortable. Until now he had not spoken to the girls. The young pioneer nurse looked into his eyes while she talked and she realized that old Jacob was smiling at her. She was nearly through with her ministering when he raised his hand feebly to acknowledge her care. He whispered hoarsely:

"To think I once told Herr Berger it was too bad for him that he could not have . . . too bad that you were girls. *Ach,* go home, *fraulein,* and tell your father that I too am happy he had daughters. Go home, tell him." The weakened old man was growing quite earnest, and Catherine could not understand the significance of what he was trying to tell her. She smoothed his brow and soothed him into late afternoon.

"There, Herr Gottlieb, there. *Ya,* I will tell my father what you say. Now my sister has warmed some soup for you. Good hot soup *mutti* made just for you." She lifted the spoonsful carefully and smiled down at her first patient.

When they ended their long trek home, their father was standing in the darkening courtyard watching for them. They waved from far off and, tired as they were, bolted for home. *"Vati, vati,* can you imagine what Herr Gottlieb was trying to tell us this afternoon? He said to tell you that he is happy that you had daughters. What did he mean?" Catherine chattered as she curled her arms around her beloved father's and looked up at him. Caroline, too, was encircled by her father's arm and was looking curious and eager.

"Vell, vell, meine kinder, old Jacob is a good friend, at last. I wish he were not so old and sick," said their father more seriously. "But he finally is getting to be a smart man," and then he began to chuckle. "What does he mean, my little girls? It is too old a story to remember, I think," he dodged their questions, "but what he says is that you daughters of mine are very good girls and he thanks me for sharing you with him. Pretty words, aren't they?" He squeezed his lips together laughingly so that deep ravines arched down his full cheeks. The girls peeped around him at each other and giggled.

"Hush, you females! I have a big surprise for you. I have been waiting all afternoon to tell you." He spoke with a flourish.

"What is it, *vati?"* they demanded.

"Vell, the morrow is the feast of the Assumption, is it not? I and your mother have decided to lock the door of the Inn for a few days and take you and the little ones on a nice trip." The twins were delighted. "We will get our baskets of food in the cart and go to see what there is to see at Oberammergau and, if there is time enough, we will go on to the Theresien-wiesen."

The sights with which Herr Berger chose to please his older daughters were his favorites, as well as theirs. The Passion Play given every year at Oberammergau for centuries had drawn Catherine into the divine act of sacrifice especially, not only when she witnessed the drama, but for the rest of her life. One of her deepest devotions was to the Passion of Our Lord; she never ceased to try, by reading and meditation, to plumb the depths of that sacrifice, as well as to imitate it.

One day when they were quite young, not old enough to comprehend, but old enough to remember, they had been left to buttons and broom dolls play by their mother who was needed in the tavern. In mischief they began looking for some new thing to interest them. Catherine, the leader of the two, pushed a stool to the wall and scrambled up onto the chest to knock down the cross that mother always paid so much attention to. They were making a game of trying to remove the corpus from the crude wooden cross by pulling out the nails in the hands and feet, as their gasping mother entered.

11

"Kinder, kinder, no!" she had said fiercely. Vexed, she lifted the holy thing from their hands and began to scold when Catherine tried to explain by saying, "He hurts, *mutti,* He hurts." The mother looked at the two alarmed faces turned up to her. She knew they could understand nothing of the true hurt of the cross; she herself was daily puzzled by all it meant. Their eyes were wide with horror, ready to shed tears. She thought to herself, "Why not let them get to know the cross? So young they are to even care. I wonder, will they always be this way?"

In the Theresienwiese, near the Black Forest and Munich, is the Statue of Bavaria, which was a new wonder in the 1830's. Done by the famed Ludwig von Schwanthaler, it is a gigantic hefty young woman holding a wreath high in one hand and a grounded sword in the other, while a peaceful lion stands beside her. To Hans Berger, the statue could have been one of his twin daughters, immortalized. He felt it was a work of greatness. And somehow, in his ponderings whenever he gazed at it, he never could come to answer the why of it, why he felt that his daughters, the twins, hinted at greatness. "Maybe it . . ." No, the answer never came.

Tonight all was gay. Herr Berger was only the father now. He luxuriated in the life and admiration of his two half-grown daughters. The three of them decided to run with the brisk breeze out onto the favorite hill walk under the bank cliff high above Arber-lake. The grass waved in the night wind. Bells rang in the distance. Hans lifted up his big feet lumberingly, but he set the quick pace. It was a grasping back for youth which he fully enjoyed. Catherine and Caroline, stretching their short legs to keep up and shouting boisterously, were ecstatic. They had this adorable innkeeper, the father who always nestled them, comforted them, aided them; they had him all to themselves.

Sometime early in the dawn, Catherine awoke to her mother's screams. Wild, loud, hysterical screaming. She hurried to be aware, to understand what might be wrong. She shook Caroline, asleep beside her, then ran to her parents' room. She saw her always calm *mutti* sobbing incoherently, her face buried in the covers of the bed. Catherine looked to her father for an explanation. Then she saw him, still with eyes shut, peacefully sleeping, dead.

Caroline crouched beside their mother but was too heart-broken to be of help. "Someone must be strong now," young Catherine told herself vaguely. "Better to let them cry themselves out now. The hard time is to come." Trembling all over, she threw her mother's shawl over her long sleeping gown and fled for *Herr Dokter* and the *Dompfarrer*.

The long, solemn funeral procession wound through the streets of Regen to the moaning strains of *Requiem aeternam dona eis Domine*. The bustling village was sorrowing, shocked at their good friend's death. Frau Berger and her two eldest daughters led the funeral queue. She leaned most heavily on them and walked unwillingly. She asked herself, "Why? Why? Why? Never time to say goodbye, to tell me what to do. He was such a good man. We have tried so hard..."

Catherine, beside her mother, was tense and immovable in her face. "Calm yourself, *mutti*. You must." She whispered with intensity. "We are having bad times but with God's help it will all work out." She was to repeat this many times in other difficult times ahead though she could not know it. She saw her mother as a terribly hurt woman, who was unable to accept this fact of death. Wasn't death but a real beginning? The thing that we spend our lives preparing for? That's what her parents and her teachers had been saying for these many years, she thought to herself as she plodded along in the new grimness.

"I need you, Katy, I need you," her mother had mumbled over and over then and later when the time came for all the family and business details to be cared for. Decisions had to be made rapidly, without time to ponder. And time and again Catherine found herself the only one able to make a decision. She did only what she knew she must do. The business must be carried on, for the family had no other means of support. Her mother could not do it alone. So young Catherine announced to her family one day soon after the funeral of her beloved father that she preferred to remain at home, not to return to the Ursulines' school with Caroline, as she had previously planned. Her mother heard the news

13

with relief. Her confusion began to lift. Caroline, it was agreed, needed to finish her secondary courses if she were to qualify as a teacher as she desired.

In their fourteenth year when the Berger twins separated, their childhood vanished, their pretty world crumbled. Caroline devoted herself to her secondary schooling and followed through with her intention by entering the English Institute of the Blessed Virgin Mary upon graduation in her eighteenth year. Catherine with her mother was allowed to attend the investiture ceremonies of Sister Xaveria, as Carolyn was named, and glowed with pride in her accomplished sister, feeling some vicarious pleasure from the impressive ritual itself. She realized completely that her sister was gone now, but the first separation long ago had hurt the most. Now, she reminded herself, she must wait. There were duties here; she could not leave her mother. Her dear mother depended on her. But the time would come; the little Maria and Johanna would take over. That day as they returned to Regen in their cart, Catherine's mother took her hand. *"Mein* Katy. I thank God for you," she said. "You made me go on when your father died," she raised her head back and pushed it down into her shoulders. Her eyes closed tightly for a moment. "You are like your father. You wear responsibility well."

In spring of 1855, Catherine honored her thirty-second birthday working in the warmth and protection of her own home, the Inn, with a large group of friends who had grown to cherish her as a friend and a dispenser of hospitality unbounded, of unfailing humor and understanding. She filled the roles of host, hostess and *sennerin* at once. While she saluted the intermittent "Prosit, *Fraulein* Katy," she moved with becoming dignity among the tables in her mother's business, seeing to the wants of their customers. "The no longer young *fraulein* was a noble woman in the town," it was often whispered. "Strange that she is not a *frau* this long time."

Catherine Berger was solid, even thickly built as a grown woman. Her eyes were large and penetrating though seldom penetrated. To all she seemed gay and outgoing, but unlike many

14

women who cared for the wants of others publicly, she was always gentle and soft-spoken. She was as happy as she could make herself be just to have the opportunity to see the smile of satisfaction come to a customer's face on being well cared for. The board and bar were still plentiful at the Berger Inn. When the time for merriment came, such as the occasion of another birthday anniversary for the oldest daughter of the house, Katy still loved to roust, to sing and dance, to be light-hearted.

Secretly, Catherine thought of time. It was a vanishing thing and threatened to crush her dream of giving herself to God. Instead, one by one, she had had to take into her daily routine not only the tasks left her by her father, but also the housekeeping and management chores which her mother was now too much an invalid to do. Her much younger sisters could have helped, of course, but like everyone else they depended on her too much to take care of everything.

Catherine did not mind any of the work. Like her mother before her, she knew she had a great capacity for work. But impatience gnawed at her. She buoyed herself up today as every day with the calm knowledge that her life was being directed by God. She attained a level of faith that allowed her to devote all her energy to the task at hand instead of wasting much of it in useless anxiety.

"This waiting doesn't alarm me nearly so much as *mutti's* determination that I must marry and spend my life here. How many times has she tried to arrange a 'match' these past fifteen years," fretted the tired woman. "I'm cross," she chided herself and began to close the festivities for the night.

Later, as she was washing dishes alone, she wondered if perhaps her mother had exhausted her efforts of marrying her off. "I know somehow that being a wife and mother is not to be my way," she mused. "But can I bear this terrible loneliness?"

Once when she was a little girl, her mother had spoken to her of her heavenly father, God. Always after that her father had been a picture to her of what God looked like. When her father died, Catherine first felt this cross of loneliness. Her father had been her idol. She had turned in desperation to the special patron of the family, to the head of the Holy Family, to the foster father of the Baby Jesus, St. Joseph. It was a logical choice for Catherine, for the saint is distinguished for his charity and patience which were her own special virtues. The events of her life, which took place long before the promises of Fatima were made in 1917 in which the devotion to St. Joseph as all-powerful after Jesus and Mary is demanded, bear splendid witness to the power of her paternal intercessor.

Catherine thought of her sister Caroline already made the superior of a school in Patna, India. A missionary. She was gone forever now. Her sister Maria whose growth she had watched eagerly in hopes that it might release her to leave as Caroline had done, was long since a bride and had made Catherine an aunt three times. Even Johanna was a well-educated, married frau of 21 years of age. "And poor *Mutti.* As the buds blossom, the bloom drops away it seems." Even walking was difficult for her now and the steep stairs almost impossible. "Really, *mutti* is the only one that holds me here now. *Ach,* what a terrible thought. I must not let myself think that my own dear mother is the one thing that stops me from attaining my soul's desire." Suddenly she looked up and realized something new that brought with it peace.

"Why, here I am stubbornly pushing for the thing I think is what I ought to do with my life when I may be all wrong from the start. This work, being here in Regen, caring for *Mutti,* perhaps that is what I am meant to do. . . . *Mein Gott,* forgive me. I accept your will."

Weary, she ascended the steps and paused by her mother's door to see if she were awake. She opened the thick carved door gingerly, for it was deeper into the night than usual. Her mother was waiting for her, trying to keep up with her sewing, which she was noted for in the community.

"Come, my dear Katy," she called thinly. "Was it a good party for you they had? I knew of it from Johanna. I was enjoying the music and noise all the way up here."

"*Ya, mutti,* it was fun. Everyone is so kind. We have many good friends. It was a good birthday. I just wish I could have had you downstairs dancing too."

16

"*Nein,* I am better off here," replied the old woman in a tone of resignation that seemed unusual to her daughter. "I have a special present for you this day. Oh, don't be expecting me to pull out another flirtatious *dirndl* that you won't wear. This is something I should have given you long years ago, but I tried to blind myself to your wishes even while I was demanding all your love and labor." She looked deeply into her daughter's face while the daughter silently, apprehensively, bent over the sewing box to arrange it. "What is *mutti* trying to tell me?" she wondered.

"Catherine, my dearest daughter, go. You have my blessing. Go. Be the nun you want to be. Give yourself to God as you want. God knows I have kept you to myself too long already. Forgive me. But it was hard for me to understand." She was crying. Catherine bent over and held her tightly in her arms. The yoke had lifted. She was free.

After a moment she began to speak quickly and her thoughts of a moment ago fell away and melted with suddenly devolved plans for her new life. She would apply immediately to the new small community of Holy Family sisters at Pirmasenz nearly two hundred miles away. The convent house was close-by her sister Caroline's motherhouse, but far different. Small, struggling, simple, devoted to charity, even living on charity alone. She would be a nun of St. Francis' Third Order, devoted to humility, poverty, simplicity. She would not really change her life although she did not realize it. She would only continue serving others in a new way. Perhaps it is providential that Catherine was forced to wait before giving herself to the community life when we see that had she entered earlier the small convent of Franciscan rule would not have existed, nor would its guiding measure of charity have been the rule for Catherine's future.

The *gasthaus* sold quickly giving Frau Berger more than enough for a long life. Catherine's chief concern at this time was arranging for her mother's care. With the counsel of her sisters and her mother, the decision as to where *mutti* would go to live was settled. Katerina Berger was quite pleased with the idea of spending her final days in a holy house and being cared for by the good sisters at the Home for Aged on Tanner Road nearby in Metten.

The entire family except Caroline were together for the fare-wells that all suspected would be long-lasting. Catherine did not leave her home and friends easily, nor did they loose their embraces without deep emotion. The moment had come. The hopeful Catherine alone waved goodbye as she left for her new home.

CHAPTER THREE

She Considered a Field and Bought It

T HE INFANT railroad line headed northward and westward from Munich through Berlin to Paris, its cars jostling along their iron treads. The openness of its two elongated wooden boxes gave the motley group of travelers aboard every opportunity to observe the wondrous workings of the novel steam engine. Coal smoke settled on the adventurous group, mostly men of professional rank. The chores of engineer and engine rivalled conversation almost as much as the very coming of the railroad rivalled the thriving coach lines of the day. Gradually the group settled back into concentrated curiosity.

Unlike her fellow passengers, the black figure that once was Catherine Berger, had shifted in her seat to look backwards and to become totally engrossed in the sight of the disappearing mountains. The signs of war in 1866 were everywhere. "Poor Bavaria," she thought, "caught up in this continual rivalry. She and Austria are no match for William and Bismarck." Her outward calm failed to hint at the melancholy that clutched at her heart. Only the stillness of her eyes, so fully gathering in the colors and shapes of her homeland, betrayed the uncertainty that now was her life; those eyes softened and strengthened by black, guard-like brows in imitation of the protection generated to the soul of the woman by a powerful Being Whom she would have humbly acknowledged as her Lord. At last the horizon altered, and the small, sturdy woman turned to face the mild wind which forced back here eyelids. She held herself erect in a docile way. On her face was an unconscious smile; over her was the habit of contentment.

Had anyone inquired, the pleasant *religieuse* would have, rather than identify herself as a daughter of Regen, Bavaria, announced that she was a Franciscan nun of the Holy Family order in Pirmasenz, part of Straubing. "I am Sister Mary Odilia," she would have spoken in a clear, soft voice. Then she would have laughed with the inquirer and agreed that her name was unusual and explained that she was given the name of an English girl who had earned sanctity through martyrdom in the first century. "A young girl I am pleased to honor and to try to imitate," she would have added humbly.

To the eye of an old friend the small convent-bound woman, who had been the jovial, hard-working Katy Berger, would have seemed much slimmer than before, graceful, impossibly calm. The mysterious aura that refines and ennobles the aspiring novice had thoroughly penetrated the being of the simple fraulein. Her lovely brown eyes were even more intense, yet comfortable in their obscurity. Beside her in the fledgling coach Sister Alberta bent over her beads, offering up the sadness that she too was feeling. She also was struggling to adjust to the certainty that she would never be able to go home again while being unassured that a secure future lay ahead. The whiffs of ascending smoke caught both of them in its meaning; their eyes as well as their spirits looked up.

In the haze Sister Odilia saw again the convent of the Holy Family nuns, the convent she had planned to call home for all the rest of her days. "So wrong I was," she shrugged. During those rushed days before her entry she had become intimate with the shambles that served the dozen devoted women as both a home and a headquarters for all their incoming and outgoing charities. It was a shabby-storied frame building, old, unadorned, devoid of exterior character. The good nuns had nurtured a *laissez-faire* attitude toward termites and elements alike chiefly because they were too completely occupied with more important details to really notice. There was the constant concern of the hungry who

20

knocked on their door for food and clothing; there was the consuming desire to render love and devotion to the Divine Master of the house; there was, inevitably, the stern monsters Poverty and Hunger to placate day after day. These things the young woman had known before she made her solemn entry between the portentous iron arches that established the scanty courtyard of the convent.

She recalled that day eleven years ago when she had passed from the secular world. Within her new home she found a warmth to her spirit that she had not found in the world of nature. Along with the precepts of this life of religion which she was embracing came new understanding of the meaning of loving and the giving of herself. Her chosen order existed on the austere vow of entrusting itself entirely to Divine Providence and living solely on the alms which were given it freely by its friends in the world. She saw the arrangement as an excellent uniting of the two worlds. The order clung to the spirit of true penance first practiced by St. Francis and imitated by the first Franciscan sister, St. Clare and her band of virgins in the 12th century who, together with Christ, had walked barefoot, observed perpetual abstinence, and made poverty the basis of their lives.

"To be a part of this unbelievably great thing, to be so privileged as to share the torturtes and triumphs of saints. This union alone," Catherine had realized as she meditated often in her postulancy, "is enough to heal the hurt of leaving Regen and *mutti* and all the family."

She had spent a year working, praying, studying within the convent walls. The final transition from her old way of life into the way of a spouse of Christ came for her and, ironically enough, for her companion, Sister Alberta, also, a year after they had entered. They had withdrawn under the inspiration of their retreat master, who was Father Joseph Nardini, the very founder of the Holy Family order, to make their first retreat. It lasted four long days. Father had made charity the theme of the retreat, Catherine remembered. "Charity, the love of God and of our neighbor for God's sake. Charity . . . is kind, is not self-seeking . . . knoweth no bounds." It fired the budding vocation with a purpose and a direct

21

goal from which, she purposed, never to wander. The climax of the retreat had come when the two women were clothed in the habit of the order, an opaque wool dress, full skirted, with a cape that fell well below the waist to cover her arms which were equally well wrapped in the wool. At the neck of the habit was a stiff bib of white over which fell the flounce and bow tie from the close-fitting matching black bonnet, edged in white. Though Catherine could not know it, the habit would last her longer than the life it then represented.

Her heart and soul had thrilled with the anthem "Te Deum" which marked the end of her formal investiture. "Holy God, we praise Thy Name." She vowed, in her promises to obedience, chastity, and poverty, to praise His Name as well all the days of her life. And she would, in a way least expected.

The transition for Catherine from her old way of life to being Sister Mary Odilia, a black garbed nun, was not the ordeal she had expected it would be. Her admired superior, Mother Joseph, too, was surprised at the vigorous way in which the new sister, much older than the usual novice, had taken up her new life. The Mother had prepared herself for the task of hard discipline to undo the many years of independence and self-concern which she had supposed Fraulein Berger had fallen prey to. But she was pleased at the docility and obedience which radiated from the strong woman who was hardly younger than herself. Through the years of mutual struggle Mother Joseph often called Sister Odilia to her for counsel. The experience the newer nun had gained in managing the affairs of the Inn as well as in handling people were a much-needed asset to the impoverished community.

Not many months after the woman from Regen had professed herself to her divine Spouse in 1862, Mother Joseph sent for her. Their momentous conference was conducted, as was all business pertaining to the convent life, in a tiny alcove off the makeshift chapel of the sisters' house, where Father Nardini sat for the sisters' confessions. Entering, Sister Odilia lowered herself as directed to a stool at her Superior's feet. "Sister Odilia, I have tried to keep the fact of our continual struggle for existence away from the other sisters, but I know you are aware of it," she began. "I have prayed

22

hard over a decision that I know I must make. Pirmasenz is not a rich community. There are many holy houses in this part of the country, so we cannot expect any more generosity from the people here than we are getting. But we must have more space and more food and supplies especially for our little orphaned children who depend on us. So I have decided that we must go out from our own country to ask for help. I want you to do this hard thing for us, Sister." She dropped her clasped hands into her lap and looked into the round, open face of her charge. She watched Sister Odilia bow her head and pull her hand to her lips characteristically.

"I have chosen you, Sister, to go through all Germany and France to beg for all the rest of us sisters and the poor people and the orphans we aid here. I realize, my child, that it is not pleasant to your nature to go about strange streets begging, but it simply must be done for . . ."

"Oh, but Mother, I am happy to do as you say," Sister Odilia intercepted. "It does seem like a very big job, though, and I do not know if I am able to . . ."

"Of course, you are. You speak French, and you are used to independence. You may take one other sister here to be your helper and companion. I will leave the choice to you. Perhaps Sister Alberta . . ."

"Yes, Mother, I would like it to be Sister. We have been working together ever since we entered. This surprises me so that I am not sure what I should do. . . . I love the life here so deeply, the prayer . . ."

"My dear, I understand," her superior answered. "But you will not lose any of your spiritual life if you do this in a spirit of obedience. And you can always have just as much solitude as you wish in your heart. Always give good example, my child, on these trips and if you are refused or insulted, accept the humiliation as did our patient Christ." The words of her holy directress sank into the obedient sister's will.

Soon after, Sister Mary Odilia, accompanied by Sister Alberta, left the community to become a mendicant. In a small valise the Sisters carried with them was a testimonial letter from their confessor and beloved founder, Father Nardini, which they offered frankly to whomever they met, hoping always to find a generous heart. The letter read:

> I, the undersigned, Deacon and Superior, testify that the holders of this, Sisters Odilia and Alberta, belonging to the Sisters of the Holy Family of the Third Order Regular of St. Francis in Pirmasenz, have been sent to collect alms for the founding of a refuge for orphans with the help of Almighty God, Who will repay a hundredfold what is given in Christian charity.
>
> (Signed) D. Joseph Nardini

Suddenly the slow-moving train held back once, twice, and began the rhythmical spasm of pulling to a stop. Jolted, Sister Odilia returned to the present. She noticed her companion, Sister Alberta, startle also. "I've been lost in remembering our very first trip together, Sister," she said quietly. "Has it been such a long time? Rough as this train is, we've certainly been used to worse ways of getting across Europe, haven't we?" The pair of black-robed women laughed together knowingly.

"We must be in France already," Sister Alberta suggested. "I didn't notice that we'd crossed the border." After a moment she continued to her dear friend, "I too was indulging in the comfortable past, Sister Odilia. We certainly have been thrown into some strange situations. How frightened I was that day in Munich when the old man we thought needed help tried to grab our bag. And yet you were not afraid to talk right up to him." Sister Odilia chuckled softly.

"It was easy, really; I have fallen so into the habit of talking boldly to my dear St. Joseph."

"You remind me of St. Theresa, honestly," said her companion. "You know how she used to scold God, telling Him it was no wonder He had so few friends the way He treated them."

"Just a woman's nature," replied the quiet friend. Sister Odilia was unhappy to have any conversation settle on herself and was already deep in the habit of keeping what was in her heart and mind solely for communion with God and her favorite, St. Joseph.

24

"And remember the dear woman who saw it all and took us home with her . . . to her castle? The great pattern of it all! *Ach, my.*" Sr. Alberta went on, realizing that with Sister Odilia to lean on she could do any hard thing that might come to her now because of this certainty in her heart that God was with them.

"I can't forget," she continued to reminisce, "the hardships of all those trips we made — how many have we made in these last five years now? The aches and pains I can always take, but you know I came from . . . my home, that is, well, it was not easy for me to go out begging, Sister." Sister Alberta was downcast. "It was not so hard when we were in our own country, but to walk so far when there was no money to ride, to go up into Prussia where the people are so antagonistic, and then . . ."

"Oh, I do understand. I felt just as you did when we were cursed at and called paupers, Sister. But how else could we be as St. Francis was? After all, we know how to count it all perfect joy," Sister Odilia said firmly.

"Yes, for dear Jesus, perfect joy," whispered Sister Alberta.

Sister Odilia spent the remaining miles trying to see how this trip fit into the broad view of their first visit to Paris, just six months ago when they went to the chancellery to obtain permission of the ecclesiastical superiors, as they were bound by their rule to do, before soliciting alms. The Archbishop of Paris was Georges Darboy, a very learned man who had written much and made a translation of "The Imitation of Christ." An energetic giant, he espoused the clerical independence of priests and holy women. Archbishop Darboy's attempt to suppress the Jesuits, and indeed all religious communities within his diocese, was not yet known by Sister Mary Odilia.

He had greeted the mendicant women from Bavaria warmly and rather than give them freedom to beg in his large province, he tried to persuade them to settle in Paris and devote themselves to helping him fulfill a long cherished dream of establishing a home for young girls of German descent.

"The fields for charity here in Paris are unlimited," he told the two travel-weary nuns. He discerned the gentle strength and ability of the spokesman, Sister Odilia. He indulged himself into

25

confiding to her his tales of need. In turn, Sister Mary Odilia was overwhelmed by this renowned man of God's confidence in her and she was moved to help him in some way. She answered his plea with the most she had to offer, "We will convey your request to our mother superior in Pirmasenz, Your Grace. I am sure she will find some way to fill this need."

"Go home, *now*," the Archbishop advised, "and ask your good superior to send me a few sisters to do this important work." Sister Odilia, whose whole being was keyed to obedience, felt that this call from the Archbishop was her task at hand and, upon leaving the Archbishop's residence, decided to abandon the remaining tour she had planned and return to the Holy Family convent as soon as possible with what funds they had collected and this vital message for Mother Joseph.

The situation at home since the two sister's last departure had deteriorated. Even before the messengers from Paris arrived at Pirmasenz they had been made aware that their roots were being shattered. Two months before, the holy man, Father Nardini, had been snatched away by death from the congregation he had founded and guided. In addition, all of Bavaria was cowering under the ominous threat of national bankruptcy thanks to the extravagance of their darling king, Ludwig II. The fate of a community of nuns dedicated to subsisting on charity when the nation itself was poverty stricken was dark.

The answer to the Archbishop's request that burned fiercely in Sister Odilia's heart was that there were no funds, much less funds to establish a far off house in Paris, France.

"The truth is, Sister," Mother Joseph told her sadly, "we are nearly lost ourselves. I know there is much work to be done in Paris, everywhere, but how can we do more than we are doing, when we struggle to keep from starving ourselves? I am not sure what is God's will any more. We have been told to separate. I do not know what will come of us sisters. . . ." Sister Odilia watched in shocked silence as clouds settled over her dear Superior's face. "Perhaps you would want to leave us. If that is so, I will give you my permission and my blessing. It might be better for you to go to Paris and start anew. The Archbishop will help you, I'm sure. After all, that is what he seems to be asking. I am so sorry that I cannot fill your purse when you and Sister Alberta kept us together 'til now financially with your trips. . . ."

Sister Odilia had spent long hours pondering this problem of where her life was to go from then on as she knelt in the chapel, completely submerged in the presence of her Almighty One. She was not one to be shaken by decision, by hard times, or by new and looming tasks. Knowing now what the situation was at home, she was troubled whether she would remain with her beloved Sisters here and try to keep them together or whether she should follow the command that beckoned her so forcefully.

She could not know that in Paris she would not find the encouraging spirit she had in enthusiasm attributed to the episcopacy. In his need to carry out his own ministering to his flock Archbishop Darboy looked for devoted women to carry through his single-minded plans. He frowned on their desire to band together, to establish the common life. He was an independent cleric; he proudly stood alone if his way alone seemed right; he had strongly opposed the passage of the dogma of papal infallibility at the twentieth Ecumenical Council. He was a strong man, certainly a holy man, who devoted his strength to carrying out his principles.

The decision had been reached painfully and sorrowfully by Sister Odilia and she was relieved to find Sister Alberta anxious to be a part of the new work. Together they had discussed their plan with Mother Joseph as they were preparing to leave. She decided it would help for her to communicate with the Archbishop himself to try to make the way as easy as possible. She spoke to them of God's designs for them. At last, she gave them news that brought joy to the apprehensive nuns' souls; she told them that two more sisters from the convent wished to be part of the Paris adventure and would follow when Sister Odilia was ready for them. It was October, 1866, when the hard way became still harder for the middle-aged nun. At forty-three, Sister Odilia was to become Mother Odilia, leading an order she knew nothing about, embarking on a strange mission with neither experience nor funds. "Thy will, not mine, be glorified," was her signpost. Now she was a different sort of a nun, bound by a vow of obedience, but to whom?

"There it is," announced Sister Alberta, nudging her. "The Paris signpost. We have arrived." The other nun nodded. She looked ahead and saw only a mountain of work. She was eager to throw herself into it.

CHAPTER FOUR

She Hath Planted a Vineyard

O<small>N THE</small> feast of St. Margaret Mary, 1866, Father Victor Braun met the meek pair of sisters at the Paris depot. *"Bon jour, mes soeurs!"* he shouted affably. A tall, thin man of forty-three years, he drew them away from the confusion and explained that he had come as a representative of Archbishop Darboy, who was most pleased with their coming and wished to see them immediately. As they walked, the priest spoke rapidly to them in French which left Sister Alberta confused and Sister Odilia not as comprehending as she would have liked.

"I, too, have felt the need for a house where working girls, German girls, if you like, could live together—safe in this wicked city," he was saying. "I belong to the Brothers of St. Vincent de Paul, and we are organizing a group of lay women to do all sorts of works of charity that we see a need for. Of course, we are not religious. I mean we do not take vows or share a common life. We do not want to live in monasteries or convents, and if we did, His Grace, the Archbishop, would have much to say in the matter. We simply wants to do works of charity. Oh, it's new to you, I know, but you'll get adjusted soon enough. There is so much work to be done here. The good ladies who work with us are most kind and sincere," he told them.

When they arrived at a small cottage and entered, Sister Odilia was puzzled at the cluster of women not wearing any religious garb or mark of a religious in any way. "I understood

Father to say he had founded a community," she questioned to herself. "But perhaps he means for me to do it."

The women she found to be earnest and eager for direction. They were all unmarried and seemingly intent on following God's special call to give themselves to Him. They told her of many other women eager to join them in their acts of charity. Sister Odilia saw the way clearing.

The interview with Archbishop Darboy was delayed. So, in the cottage of the family of Annette Devereaux, she and Sister Alberta ended their long trek to Paris. Early the next morning she questioned the family, especially the young Annette as to how the lay communities in Paris existed. She could discover only that the group met whenever Father Braun notified them and that their work was as yet a bit disorganized. Later, when she hastened to see the prelate who had initiated her vigorous interest in establishing the home for girls, she found even Archbishop Darboy quite vague about the routine of any community Victor Braun might have founded but most enthusiastic about getting the girls' home immediately.

"I have a location for you, Sister, a big house that is in quite good repair. All you have to do is staff it and gather in the many, many young women who are crowding into Paris daily without any sort of protection. You shall call it the *Asyle du Sacre Coeur*. I am," he emphasized, "most anxious that your work should be successful."

Sister Odilia was greatly relieved with his words. "And have you any counsel for me, Your Grace, as to the spiritual order that our Sisters should follow?" she asked obediently when he had finished.

"Order? Well, Sister Odilia. Has no one informed you that I generally do not approve of going about organizing communities of women and men with this common life, vows, rules, and the like?" He spoke sternly and Sister Odilia's raised brows were the only clue that she perceived that her mighty errand was to be far different than she had hoped. "But I understand that you have lived in community life for too long a time to just cast the regularity of it aside. I give you permission to continue as you are accustomed

30

to doing. The work will be all consuming, I warn you, so that a strict routine is impossible here. But," he spoke sincerely, "it's easy for me to see that you are an exceptional person, and I will not attempt to interfere with the plans our Almighty Father has for you. Use your own judgment as you do this great work in Paris. I will try to help you all I can."

The meeting was not all Sister had hoped for. She left the chancellery with some misgivings, but the Archbishop had commissioned her to use her good judgment, which was what she would do.

One gloomy afternoon four years later Mother Odilia knelt in her tiny, bare room before her treasured replica of her dear friend, St. Joseph. It was a noble statue of sturdy, white stone nearly as old as the nun herself. It had been with her when she was a fatherless young girl in Regen, then in Pirmasenz when she was an endeavoring novice, and now here in Paris, a mother of many endeavoring novices, a Superior of a religious order for whose existence she was now offering prayers of great thanksgiving and even greater petition. The unlined face of the nun was apprehensive. As usual the way was not clear for her, but in her thoughts was a resolution to do what she felt was the Will of her Lord and Master.

"The work our Sisters do is truly of great value in this huge city of Paris," she meditated. "We have opened not only this home for working girls which we share, but with as many orphans as we can feed and crowd in share too. It's such a demanding responsibility for all of us; yet everyone gives gladly. Just to see the grateful relief written on the faces of the young frightened things when we gather them together from the streets and railroad stations is enough. Imagine our gratitude, dear Spouse of Mary, to be able to be a part of this, God's work.

"But what of the rule which I feel is so important? It often seems to me that I am so busy caring for the girls and the children, seeing that they are both spiritually and materially safe that I have no time to devote to bringing myself and the wonderful Sisters

31

who have joined us closer to you and your Son. I welcome all the crosses our dear Lord sends me. If the begging must be, then we will beg. If the sick call us to them when we are most tired, then we go happily. But if only we could know that all this work in the world is what Our Lord wants. I feel that we must have a common spiritual life, special training and discipline. Help me to do what is right, dear St. Joseph. You must."

She pulled herself up and hurried to her desk in the kitchen on the ground floor of the large house in the poorest district of Paris. Waiting for her were several important matters.

She glanced through the several letters and picked out one postmarked Metten, Bavaria, with a quickening heart. She read:

> Metten, Bavaria 1870
>
> My dear daughter,
> It hurts me bitterly that I have not had a word from you for eighteen months. It makes my heart sad to think that you have forgotten me. I have never forgotten you. I offer my most fervent prayers to God for my children daily.
> How great my sorrow was and still is at the death of my beloved Sister Xaveria. I can't explain it in words. Only a motherly heart can feel how it is to be deprived of her children.
> How I wish you could come to Metten. Please ask the Vicar General, if you could make the trip. It would please me very much to see you again.
>
> Your most devoted mother,
> (Signed) Katerina Berger.

As she folded the letter numbly and slipped it back into its envelope, Mother Odilia's body inwardly clenched. She strained to stop tears which responded to the complaint from the one person whom she never put from her prayers and intentions. And that Sister Xaveria was dead! She had not been told. Could *mutti* have forgotten such an important thing? Perhaps her mother had not meant to have her hurt when the awful news came from India . . . When? How long ago? How? The distance was too much. . . . What could she do when she was halfway across Europe from her dear mother? "To be in a strange land is cross enough," thought Mother Odilia in agony. "Caroline is with God. Her life on earth

32

ended. And my poor, poor mother. She is alone; age is breaking her heart, and I am too far away to even smooth her brow. How cruel of me that I have not written her. Can it be so long? It does not seem possible that there has never been a moment . . . but to write *mutti* I always must gather my thoughts so that I can try my best to tell her in words what love I have for her in my heart. Oh, God, God, help her, tell her now that I hold her dearly in my heart," the petition pounded in her head. "Tell her that it is Your business that takes me far away from her. Please, dear God, let her remember the happy days when she feels the most desolate. And I shall write her yet today." But the tidings of this first letter left Mother Odilia inwardly stunned. Caroline, whose being intertwined with her own for the happiest part of her life, was dead. It was hard to realize.

The remaining letters had come in reply to a request of the ever-watchful Mother who was concerned for the safety of her young Sisters whom she was forced to send on missions of charity into far places. Even though the sisters were not as impoverished in Paris as the Holy Family sisters in Pirmasenz had been, they still found it necessary to collect alms to support their works of charity. Thus, Mother sought letters of recommendation. Bishop George Anton of Wurzburg, Germany, wrote:

Wurzburg, 21 March

George Anton, through the mercy of God and the Grace of the Apostolic Chair, Bishop of Wurzburg. After His Majesty, the King, gave his permission to Mother Odilia from Straubing, Directress of the "Asyle du Sacre Coeur" in Paris, we allow her after having proof of the very successful work of that institution, to take up collections for the duration of four months through the entire kingdom. This may be published through any article in the daily paper also through personal delegation of two members of her institution. This work is fully recommended to the charitable mind of the members of the Diocese.

The second came from the Minister of Bavaria appointed to Paris, Baron de Perglat:

Paris, 15 November

The undersigned Minister of Bavaria, certifies by Mother
Odilia, superior of the Servants of the Sacred Heart, 25 Hum-
bolt Street, Paris, that this work of charity designed to save
working girls from falling into evil is favorably known in
Paris and that she can in all conscience be recommended to
Christian charity.

(Signed) Baron de Perglat,
Legation de Baviere, Paris

The testimonials brought some relief to Mother's overwhelmed mind this autumn day. She bowed her head momentarily.
Suddenly the door swung open and Sister Magdalene Fuerst, newly
in charge of the orphans, crept in shyly. *"Excusez-moi, ma mere,"*
she began. Mother Odilia had recognized the flint of maturity in
the young girl, who came to her three years ago when the work of
establishing the house to care for the charitable cases directed to
them by Father Victor and the Archbishop was floundering. She
was unusually young, Mother had reflected, but the attraction of
the little ones to her and of her toward them was remarkable.
She had gradually increased the girl's responsibilities until the day
when she professed formally her desire to be a religious and took
the name of her mother. And now Mother Odilia looked upon the
harassed young nun with loving concern. It was moments like this
when her memory darted back to her novitiate days when she had
had doubts about her ability to bear the loss she felt she must sustain by not having children of her own. Clearly, the words of her
novice mistress-mentor returned to her, "All the world will be
your children." She chuckled, a little bewildered at the miracle.
Sister Magdalene took the smile to be an indulgent one and with
more courage said:

"It's the new boys, Mother. There are four brothers that
were brought to us this morning and the oldest is like a father to
the others although he is only nine years old himself. I wish they
could all be kept together in the same room. Their parents are
gone and they are pathetically lost. Only the big brother seems to
be able to help them right now."

34

"Same room? Alone, you mean, Sister? Well, why don't we give them the storage room next to the dormitory on the third floor? We can clear out what's there and put out the mattresses and feather ticks that Father Victor sent over last week. That way the four of them can get used to the other children gradually. And why don't you look for some warm coats for the poor things? One of the good ladies that comes to help mentioned to me yesterday that she had brought a bundle to us, and I asked her to put them in the community room."

"Oh, yes, Mother, I shall. And just as soon as my new boys are used to us I will move them into the dormitory with the other children. Then we will have more room still . . ."

"You daughters of charity," chided her Superior affectionately. "How shall I keep up with you?"

"I realize what a constant struggle it is for you, Mother Odilia," the young sister consoled her hesitantly. "Forgive me for being bold but even though our orphans' home does cost so terribly much, and none of the children have anyone to give us any money to help care for them, still they are so adorable, so eager to take and return love. Why just to cuddle them. . . ." She was weeping in her intensity. "Just look, Mother, one of the older children showed me this poem which he found being distributed to the people in the city. He said it made him feel just like telling the world about how much he loved you. Read it, Mother. I think it's so lovely."

Mother Odilia picked up the dingy papers and began to read the verses written by she knew not whom:

To Mother Odilia

Who goes from house to house
With praise greeting
Goes so happy in and out
With never tiring foot?

Black veil covers the head
Crucifix on breast
This testifies to whom they are betrothed
And believe and serve with holy joy.

On the girdle hangs the rosary
In the hand a collecting sack

In rain as in sunshine
They walk through the land.
They say "Praised be Jesus Christ"
Have mercy for His sake.
I collect where there is love left
For His poor.

Everybody of free desire
His little gift brings
In this way the old Christian love
Will for long be renewed.

Therefore, poor sister, walk on
Collecting without stop or rest
Until from place to place you find
A heart for God.

When at last you come to your Bridegroom
As victims for thy duty
Too soon arrived at the end
Forget not the giver.

Sister Alberta rushed in while Mother was still perusing the amateurish tribute. Mother rose from the table in faint alarm and steeled herself for her fellow Bavarian sister's message.

"Mother, it has come," Sister Alberta announced triumphantly. "At last our prayers are answered." She was breathless. Mother Odilia's face became radiant. She knew that St. Joseph had been busy as she had asked, and had supplied them with a spiritual father to care for their present daily needs. She clasped her hands in joy and went to embrace her beloved message-bearer.

"I finally got in to Archbishop Darboy with your requests, and I found him surrounded with military attachés and workers of every kind. In the scant moment we spoke he said he understood our needs and then went to his desk and signed this note for you. One of his aides explained the confusion to me. He said that the Archbishop is organizing all the relief for the wounded that he can. Hospitals, nursing crews . . . it was all quite exciting, but at last. . . ."

"You bring all sorts of news, Sister Alberta," Mother responded. "I am filled with joy at this moment to think that now all our efforts to care for God's creatures can be crowned with

36

simple vows and the spiritual routine of St. Francis. And we shall have our own confessor for strength and counsel. Did His Grace designate anyone in particular to us when you spoke to him, Sister?"

"No. But at least it will not be Father Braun, Deo Gratias," she chanted.

"Hush, please, sister. We must remind ourselves that God's Will will be done." Mother Odilia was disturbed that any unpleasantness should invade the sisters' house which could now, she realized, he called a convent. "A great goal has been reached for all of us. Let us give thanks to Our dear Lord Who watches over us and leads us."

"Yes, Mother," Sister said penitently.

"Your news, Sister, that the Archbishop is trying to help the French troops brings the war with Prussia very close. How very sad it is. Our own country, Bavaria, is forced into war again in defense of our unkind neighbor, Prussia. All of us here are in a very sorry situation, for we are, strictly speaking, enemies of the French, since we are native Germans."

Through her busy schedule, Mother Odilia was always alert to reports concerning not only the city of Paris but all of France and, more especially of Germany, and Bavaria, her own country.

In 1870 when war between France and Prussia had been declared, she had spoken to her Sisters of the momentous event. Austria, which had recently fought to maintain itself against a traditional rivalry with Prussia, now sided with France against the Prussians.

Prussia on the other hand was justly defending itself now against Napoleon III's aggression. The Prussians would shrewdly survive the clash and would emerge as an empire, having been joined finally by the southern German states — Bavaria among them — who gave up their independence reluctantly. Ironically, the French Empire would decline after its defeat.

"I find it difficult to call myself a German who have been an independent Bavarian all my life," Mother declared to the Sisters. "Ah, well, surely, in our nursing there will be some way in which we can work with Archbishop Darboy in this good work of his.

Excuse me, Sisters, I am going to find Sister Gervaise and speak to her about it."

Mother's girlhood experience with her own mother at caring for the sick opened her eyes to the hidden illnesses and constant needs of the poor people of Paris. She had never been able to refuse help, so she had pressed herself into every effort to make the infinite charity of Him Who led her known as widely as possible. Sister Gervaise had been her special aide in this and stood as dispenser of medicines and bandages over the constantly depleted and replenished supply. Many times the two of them had visited homes to bathe and care for the invalids and diseased until their baskets were empty. Then together they would make their return home a begging tour which gave them something to work with on the morrow.

After Mother had left them, Sister Magdalene smiled at Sister Alberta and the older nun said, "I should never have brought Father Victor into our conversation just then." And she shook her head in vexation.

"No matter how exasperating that man is, Mother always ignores it and just plods along trying to do what's right," agreed Sister Magdalene. "Why, if he had his way, there would still be no place for the poor children here and we would not even be helping the sick."

"You're right, Sister. But Father Victor sees these needs just as Mother does. It's just that he is very slow and cautious, almost reluctant, to act where Mother is so efficient and selfless that if she sees something needs to be done, immediately she starts working out a way to do it. Of course, Father Victor resents her immensely because he feels he should be our leader. The situation worries me, but Mother is too busy to notice, I think."

Later in the day Mother was coming into the house from being with the children in the play yard. Sister Marie Anne met her and said that Father Braun was in the parlor and wished to see her immediately. Mother accepted the news casually, for throughout the four years of working with the priest there had been countless occasions for conferences between them. The thought that perhaps with this new permission from the Archbishop, Father Braun might see fit to arrange for Holy Mass to be said in their convent house was most prominent in Mother's mind. She would speak to him about it now. Once in the presence of the cleric, however, she realized that something serious was amiss. He was pacing back and forth around the room, an angry scowl on his face. He immediately came toward her and, shaking his finger menacingly, he shouted:

"Such haughty, domineering conduct I have never seen in all my life, never, never, never! To go to the Archbishop over my head when I am the founder of this house!"

Mother Odilia raised her hand in horror at such anger and her jaw dropped uncomprehendingly. She could not speak.

"I made you Superior of my order and now you are seeking the veneration and filial respect which the Sisters had promised only to me, their Father Founder. You are attempting to destroy this entire congregation and have actually, behind my back, succeeded in winning the Archbishop over to your side. It's despicable. You, Mary Odilia Berger, are to leave this house and never come back."

The priest was in a rage and, fortunately, decided that the thing to do now was to go himself to see the Archbishop and make his pronouncement official. He thundered from the house leaving behind a gathering audience of small eager children and wide-eyed nuns aghast.

Mother Odilia was reeling under this latest and most bewildering blow. She could feel the words pounding like hammers on her chest, raining like hail stones on her head. Thoughts of what really had been happening, what had been so viciously misconstrued just now kept throbbing in her brain and her throat ached to speak out in self defense. She groped for a chair for support, then at last sank into it and bowed her head down upon her lap in sorrow. She sat there, a solitary figure, until long after darkness had fallen.

Recovering her senses slowly, she found herself kneeling. "Perhaps the hardest thing of all to bear without complaint is the final degradation of being falsely accused under which our Master died." The realization came to her. "How humble I feel," she mused. "Yet how close to you, my Jesus. I suppose that bearing an experience like this one could be as close to experiencing Your Divine Passion as one could ever come. What have I done? But then what did You do, dear Lord."

"Not my will but Thine," she said aloud, rising from her knees and going to her room. She tried to rationally analyze the situation, her role there, and what had gone wrong. She had known from the beginning that there was a tragic personality clash between Father Braun and herself. At first she had tried to attune herself to his ways. But as time went on, she saw more and more that the mountain of work screaming to be accomplished just was not getting near to that. Probably she had been too enthusiastic. But she knew she could not have been otherwise. It was not her nature. The four years here in Paris establishing the convent, the girls' home, and the orphanage, making the sick visits, whatever had been done was the fruit of human weakness and a pathetic instance of teamwork, she concluded.

Through the night the sorrowful woman considered her situation. Her humility and good sense led her to forego any thought of a disruptive rebellion within the religious order that she had come to love so much. As the sun was spreading its mighty beauty over the horizon, Mother Odilia sighed. The vision of greatness seemed to find her with a deeper serenity in Christ. She was, she realized, above all merely God's instrument.

Next morning, before imparting the distasteful news to her cherished Community, Mother Odilia determined to visit the man who had been responsible for the direction of her work in Paris, Archbishop Darboy. Her reception was kind and sympathetic. When she approached the Archbishop's secretary, she was moved to find that the patriarch had left word for her to be announced immediately. As she was led into the austere office which she had come during the past four years to feel was a place of Divine Presence, she saw Archbishop Darboy rise and come toward her ingratiatingly. "Sit down, please, Mother Odilia," he began. "There is no need to explain to me the purpose of this visit. I have been hoping you would come. If you had not arrived soon, I was about to send for you. This business with Father Victor is most miserable. But it has happened and I want you to feel as I do that there is a purpose in its happening."

"I believe I do, Your Grace," Mother pronounced quietly. She sat huddling with her still hands twined together in her lap. "And I fully trust in your wisdom to tell me what is to be done now. I pledged my obedience to you when Sister Alberta and I first came to Paris. And after this, I have no one but you to turn to."

"Unfortunately you are right, Mother," he acquiesced. "All property you have acquired has been deeded in the name of Father Braun and his friends. Although I wish truly that the circumstances were different, I do have an errand for you that is close to my heart. While our poor country is at war, the work done by you and your sisters cannot flourish anyway. Right now it is the troops we must think of; whether they are German, French or Austrian . . . don't you agree? Yes, well, I received word yesterday that an emergency hospital is being set up in Elberfeld in the Rhineland near the coast. You must go there and carry on your work among your own people. The injured are pouring into the little industrial town because it has the only railroad left intact with all the terrors of this war plaguing even it. There is no time to lose. I advise you to leave Paris this very day. It will be easier for you that way."

Just as he beckoned Mother Odilia to Paris because she would be useful to his own projects, Archbishop Darboy, in spite of himself, proved to be an instrument in the Divine Hand in beginning the work she would ultimately follow. Seemingly oblivious to the torment in her heart over the upheaval of her work at the convent, he commissioned her to a new far-off mission field because she would again fill a need in his special area of interest. There was no word of commiseration, nor hint of vindication from him. But Mother Odilia looked for none. There was again elation in her heart that she still could work for God and her fellow men. This new assignment was proof enough to her that God was not displeased with her efforts. Archbishop Darboy sent her off with funds for train tickets from Paris to Elberfeld, Germany, for herself and Sister Magdalene, who they both knew would not want to stay behind in Paris. From the Prelate she also took with her words of caution concerning her foreign status.

Conditions in Paris at this time were perilous. Napoleon III in splendor upon his recently created throne, was avid for power and wanted the whole European world at his feet, which could be brought about only by a war. What to war about?

In 1870, a pretext for a war was found in the Hohenzollern candidacy for the Spanish throne. Napoleon's threats met with unexpected resistance from Bismarck, minister to William I of Prussia. The French ambassador, Benedetti, was ordered to demand of King William of Prussia that he prohibit Prussian Prince Leopold from accepting the offer of the throne. The King retorted that "not having advised it, he could not forbid it." To the disappointment of Emperor Napoleon, however, the Hohenzollern Prince voluntarily declined and that way to a war seemed closed again.

The French were empire-building, nevertheless, and the coltish German Confederacy still recovering from the Austrian-Prussian war of 1866 seemed a likely first venture.

Another factor fomenting the Franco-Prussian War of 1870 was the indignation of French Catholics against protestant Prussia; first, for instigating to put a non-Catholic on the throne of traditionally Catholic Spain, and secondly, for humiliating the traditionally Catholic countries of Baden, Wuttenburg, and Bavaria in a coercive *kulturkampf* — a war between church and state — into joining the North German Confederation, formed by Bismarck in 1867.

War seemed both opportune and unavoidable.

So Mother Odilia and her companion were caught up in a double web of warring passions which made them undesirable in France because of their German nationality and undesirable in Germany because of their religious affiliations.

Yes, the Archbishop was right. What chance was there of starting a new religious community of any kind in Paris at this time, or in Germany for that matter? Being German made her odious to the Frenchmen among whom she lived. Very soon, she mused, all Germans would be deported from France. As long as she would have to leave, it would be better if she left at this time. That's what she would do. She would go back to her native country where there was work for her to do.

Coming to the convent, she resolutely called the Sisters together in the community room. Then she sketched out for them, in her simple way, the charges of Father Braun and the Achbishop's suggestion that she leave France immediately. She hushed their protestations and sorrow with the assurance that it was the Holy Will of God.

After the members of the community had received their Mother's blessing and spoken tender words of Godspeed to her, they went back to their duties, as she had asked them to do. Only one remained.

"Please, mother, may I go with you?" Sister Magdalene begged.

And Mother, grateful to God for companionship in her exile, replied, "Yes, sister, if you wish. I would have been doubly hurt to have been deserted by you, Sister Magadelene!" More lightly she said "we have no bags to pack as we are permitted to take nothing with us but the clothes we wear, according to Father Braun. So after holy Mass tomorrow, we will start out. We must go empty-handed."

CHAPTER FIVE

Her Lamp Shall Not Be Put Out in the Night

In MID-DECEMBER, 1870, the exhausted women, already haunted by the terrors of having no home and yet nowhere special to go, arrived in the city of Elberfeld, or Lippe as it was also called, to find it filled with even more confused, frightened crowds of people. The train terminal was in almost total darkness because of the fighting nearby. People were rushing around frantically. Friendly German troops seemed to have taken over the local authority. Mother Odilia grasped one young soldier by the arm and meekly asked what was happening. She learned that the train from Paris to Elberfeld, already the last to be allowed to make the long border crossing, was about to be eliminated also. The German army had erected barricades over the rails just outside the city and were now in the process of confiscating the French train and imprisoning its crew as hostages.

Mother Odilia knew that the war was becoming more intense. The realization of what caring for war casualties meant began to grow in her mind. She accepted the awful situation without pondering. She had never known the rigors of a war, and now that the time for her own participation seemed so close, she was more than content to go ahead blindly and take each new experience and revelation as it came. A respite came to her and her companion at being at least among their own countrymen once more.

The overnight trip had been gruelling with repeated military checks at every one of the many stops. Now hunger was gnawing at them; even winter made itself uncomfortably familiar through their worn and wrinkled habits. They slipped on their long cloaks and left their arrival behind, determined to find a church and some spiritual strength.

Two miles away Father Wilhelm Frederici prepared to offer his usual Mass for his scattered congregation in the only Catholic church in Elberfeld. He was a tall, gaunt Prussian with almost no hair to modify his severe features. He moved about the altar gracefully, despite his age, and was somberly absorbed in the act of his Mass. As he distributed Communion ponderously he hesitated over the pair of unfamiliar religious at his rail. What could it mean, he wondered.

Kneeling in a pew close to the front of the modest church, Mother Odilia rejoiced in her thanksgiving. With her Lord in her heart, the spirit of the humble woman who had dedicated her life to Him and who was spending her life actively doing whatever He asked of her, soared with requited love. Her moment of petition dragged her back to the painful reality of her scorned state. She could bring herself to make but one request of her God whom she knew to be more generous than demanding. "Dear Lord, let Thy Will be done. Help me to be strong enough to always know that no matter what happens, You will take care of us. She closed out the hurt of the past few days and the worry of the present with a painful effort in order that she could allow her Spouse to make his message for her heard.

The middle-aged nun knelt erect with her eyes fixed calmly on the little House on the altar. She looked drawn, her black garments were ill-fitting, indicating she was thinner than before. She smiled with unconscious pleasure at being once again in a parish church in her own land. She was not unlike the humble parish priest of Ars, France, who became a saint by travelling the difficult road of calumny and persecution and hatred. But Mother Odilia's thoughts as she knelt before the Tabernacle trying to forget another failure, about to make another beginning at forty-seven years of age, were far from likening herself to a saint.

46

It is understandable that the sight of the nuns of a strange order assisting at Mass aroused Father Frederici's interest. He was an overworked man, handling the good sized parish alone since the beginning of the war months ago. "Because of the war, too, there is even more work to be done here in Elberfeld," he thought to himself. "But for two Catholic religious women to be alone anywhere in this stirred up country is not good." He waited for the holy women at the vestibule of his church to invite them to breakfast with him.

While they waited for Father's housekeeper to finish the preparations for the morning meal, Mother Odilia surprised the priest with an immediate rush of questions about the hospital she expected to work for in Elberfeld.

"I know nothing about this hospital of which you speak, good Sister," the old man said, frowning. "How did you hear this thing," he queried.

Mother Odilia spoke of their work in Paris to identify herself and Sister Magdalene to the wisely cautious man, then she explained the cause for the disruption at the little convent house of the Soeurs Servantes. "I am a humble servant of His Grace, Archbishop Darboy," she said simply. "It is he who sent Sister and me to your city and was kind enough to pay the train fare, since we have no money of our own. We expected to be needed here, I . . ."

"Ah, now I see," Father Frederici exclaimed. "His Grace is a wonderful friend of mine. If he sent you, Sisters, do not fear. He has some plan in mind. Perhaps the timing has gone wrong. But here, please drink this boiled coffee. And we are having some delicious *kuchen* too, thanks to the thoughtfulness of *Frau* Fantropp. We will have no trouble finding charity for you good Sisters to do here in Elberfeld, believe me, hospital or no hospital." He smiled cheerfully at the women to hide his alarm. "And first, since you are penniless and there are no other sisters in this vicinity, we must find a home for you." He leaned back in his straight-backed chair and pursed his lips for a moment. "*Ach,* what is the matter with me," he said, jumping up excitedly, "I know just the place. You liked the *kuchen, ya?* Well, I shall take you to the home and the maker of our sweet cake. *Frau* Fantropp is a good, generous

47

woman. She and Emil are bakers; they live not far from here. Come, I will tell you about them and the life here as we are walking."

As she climbed the steep slope together with Sister Magdalene and their new-found friend, Mother Odilia looked back over the countryside and felt a surge of hope and enthusiasm flow into her. An hour ago in the church she had feared that the complete resignation with which she had been fortifying herself the past few days would be the last resource on which she could draw for the rest of her life. It was a thought she could only face with teeth clenched and grim determination clouding all her innate gaiety. But now, so soon she could scarcely believe it, she was eager to face life, to meet the people who would be part of her new work. Resignation she knew she must have but she could not do without the overwhelming spirit inside her to progress, to get things done, and to always do better. Mother Odilia exclaimed at the lovely view. "Your beautiful church, Father Frederici! You must work hard to keep it looking so well," she added.

"Not my church, though, good Mother," he answered. "It is St. Joseph's church. He is always a good friend to me, so I like to work hard to keep his name and his house well kept, you know."

"Why, Father Frederici, how strange you too should know dear St. Joseph so well," Mother replied. "I too have a very special love for him. He has been good like a father to me."

"Yes, it is strange," the priest repeated. "It is strange how some things happen. No matter how we try we cannot comprehend." The three walked on in silence.

It was the third week after their arrival in Elberfeld. Mother Odilia and Sister Magdalene had taken positions in the local garment factory as an immediate means of livelihood at Father Frederici's counsel. They were helping make soldiers' uniforms for Prussian and Bavarian troops. Mother rebelled inwardly at this work, which seemed to be abetting war. Yet she frequently smiled secretly over her machine at the oddness of her position now as a seamstress putting to work all the lessons learned from her mother, who in her time in Regen had been the finest of seamstresses. The conditions at the factory were rough and, because many of the workers there were men, Sister Magdalene complained of the loose masculine conversation. Again Mother offered thanks for her early days in the Inn when she was made to accept such discomfort. She made a practice of offering up the rigors of this unpleasant routine in reparation for the repeated profanations against the holy name of her Master.

Late one evening, the Sisters trudged toward the Fantropps' lighted window anxiously anticipating the lavish repast which *Frau* Fantropp always prepared for them. Their stay with these kind people renewed their spirits as well as their waistlines, Mother Odilia and Sister Magdalene frequently agreed jokingly to their hostess. They entered the small flat-stone cottage. Once inside they shed their weariness after having worked from early dawn, for the home was clean and delicious-smelling. Their two rooms upstairs were much more comfortable than any stay they had had since before entering the convent. Tonight they were pleased to see Father Frederici visited with Emil and *Frau* Fantropp. "Hello, my dear Sisters, I have been waiting for you," he said, smiling broadly. "I have good news."

Mother Odilia went forward eagerly. *"Ya, Herr Domp-farrer,* what is this news?" She held her hands together at her waist and she waited with an infectious eagerness displayed in her eyes.

"Mother, your hospital has come just as you said." He motioned the sisters to be seated, then he began his explanation. "Today the mayor of our city came to me seeking some honorable person to take charge of a military hospital that must be opened to care for all the wounded who are coming here from the battle fields all around us. The City Barracks at Brill has been turned over to him and the military command and although it certainly will not be the most ideal arrangement, it will have to do. The need is urgent. Will you come to help direct his work, Sister?"

Early the following day, Mother Odilia with Father Frederici, met with the Büergermeister and other city officials of Elberfeld and Brill. The supervision of the hospital would be left to the responsible woman, they agreed. All the medicine and supplies that were available were to be turned over to her. She would, they warned, have to make the best of what there was. No one seemed to have much knowledge of what was required in the establishment of a hospital, and the presence of an overwhelming number of sick, wounded, and dying soldiers was a problem gladly transferred to what they disconcertedly hoped were more capable shoulders.

For Mother the work of the new hospital began immediately. She and Sister returned to bid their beloved friends, the Fantropps, thank you and farewell. Then they left with Father Frederici for another new beginning.

They found the City Society Hospital, as the barracks was re-named, to be a sturdy, square building of gray stone. There were two floors of bare long rooms which were already filling up with cots lining either wall. Crowding in were distraught men of all ages, some able to walk, some delirious with pain and fever. Mother saw the men crowd beds so close together that there was no room to pass between them. It was obvious that the men had been forced to fend for themselves since being delivered from the battlefields and were happy with the most meager balm. Long narrow windows like chinks in the wall grudgingly introduced the afternoon sunlight into the miserable rooms.

Mother Odilia shivered with pity at the misery that met her gaze as she stood in the doorway. "There is work enough here," she told herself. "But where to begin?" Hurrying with Sister Magdalene to their own quarters, a separate two-room building, bare but at the same time affording them the quiet and privacy they would need, she donned an apron, rolled up her sleeves, then returned to the barracks-hospital to characteristically throw herself into the task of hospital administrator, nurse, attendant, and, perhaps most important of all, dispenser of good will and inspiration.

Returning to the hospital she found that two of the more able men had been making an effort to feed the growing numbers of wounded. She pitched in to help them and spent the rest of the first day there moving among the men, quietly delivering the bowls of lukewarm thin soup and feeding the helpless. She saw that if a wounded man was too sick to eat, he just missed that meal. There was no one to assist the patient who was too weak to sit up and help himself.

Mother would never forget those faces that first night. Varying degrees of curiosity, hate, suspicion, pain, loneliness, and stupor were shown by the men as their eyes followed her from bed to bed. The need for love and kindness was conspicuous in each face. The need for medical balm and for cleanliness was even more so.

That night she lay planning her work. She decided to collect all the less wounded first, teach them how to change bandages and beds, and assign a director of each of several wards. The sickest she would put together, those with the same sickness together. Her work was beginning to be clear in her mind. "Actually," she told herself, "this is a good idea, bringing the sick together so that more can be cared for efficiently. Imagine I who have never been in a hospital, now in charge of one! Only let me be Your instrument, dear Lord." She slipped off into sleep repeating, "St. Joseph, you must help me in this work."

Nursing the sick soldiers was a mighty task for the Sisters. Heroically, they spent all their time and strength, their skill and love for their patients in the Brill wartime institution. Bandaging the ugly gashes, assisting the doctors in their surgery, being ready with a patient smile were their new duties. The soldiers, in turn, came to accept the always giving Sisters and to anticipate their presence. The routine of the once haphazard hospital was welcomed and the sharp decrease in the death rate was noticeable enough to merit Mother warm commendations. Above all, her spirit of selflessness was as contagious as some of the diseases she came in touch with. To Father Frederici who visited the hospital to offer Mass and distribute Communion as well as to discuss the problems Mother met with in her administrative post, it seemed positively a marvelous thing to see what charity personified in the Sisters as they moved through the wards could produce in the hearts of those embittered fighting men whose lives it touched.

One day in mid-April, 1871, Father came to Mother Odilia bringing sad news from Paris. The Soeurs Servantes du Sacre Coeur, of which Mother had been superior during her four years in Paris, had been removed from Paris to Sevres, France, by Father Braun soon after Mother's departure. He had given reasons to his own order, Les Freres, that the increasing amount of work and high cost of living in Paris were insurmountable problems for the little congregation. Actually, according to Father's information, the change was made because of the new, unfriendly attitude of Archbishop Darboy toward them. More recently, the Prussian priest related, Father Braun was dismissed from his own order. It was unfortunate, they both agreed. Father Frederici also brought news that the Archbishop himself had been taken prisoner and was confined in the prison at Mazas. "This is most alarming," the priest said solemnly. "We must pray for His Grace's safety. Angry soldiers in the passion of war . . . there is no way of knowing." Mother Odilia was deeply disturbed. The Prelate had been responsible for her material and spiritual guidance for many years. To have him fall victim to the insane war was unthinkable for her.

A still more piercing blow was delivered at that time to Mother. A letter from Bavaria had been forwarded to her from Paris as had the information. Taking it, she quietly rejoiced. "It can only be from *mutti!* It is good that I wrote her early this year; with all our work coming to an end here it would be impossible to find time for it now. She must have received the *crêche* I sent her at Christmas, despite the war." Opening the envelope hastily, she began to reread the brief note. It was from her own dear *dompfarrer* in Regen, an expression of sympathy:

> Ave Maria!
> Just now, your honored mother, Catherine Berger, in the hospital, after receiving all the holy Sacraments, died of a stroke. She will be buried on the Feast of St. Stephen.
> (Signed) John Ev. Angmaher, Pastor

"The feast of St. Stephen! Mother was dying as I was beginning with the hospital. All these months she has been gone and I did not even know. The *crêche* . . ." After reading the message over several times, Mother Odilia withdrew to be alone in the Sisters' quarters. There, kneeling on the cold floor, she took out her heavy rosary and began to beseech God for the soul of her dearest Mother.

Four months after the Sisters' arrival, the fighting abated somewhat. The German army assigned enough male nurses to Brill so that the sisters' services were no longer needed, although they were invited to remain. For the apostolate which it afforded, they would have done so, but Father Frederici decided they should leave since their services could be better utilized elsewhere.

It was a sad parting. All the men insisted on saying goodbye to Mother and so she went from bed to bed and for each she had a word of encouragement. She had indeed been a mother to each and they had grown to love her. And now, she stood on the thresh-hold again! But how different from that day in the middle of December. She marveled at the change in these men. She marveled at those same eyes; yet they were not the same! Kindness, love, and prayer had filled them with a placidity that warmed her heart.

"God bless you all," she called from the doorway. With husky voices they called after her, "God bless you too, mother, and reward you for everything." She carried with her the following letter from the Büergermeister of Elberfeld:

> Ave Maria!
> This is to testify that the two sisters, Odilia and Magdalene, nursed the wounded soldiers in the City Society Hospital at Brill from December 1870 until April 20, 1871. Their sacrificing spirit, their untiring care of the sick and wounded by day and night deserves the highest praise.
> May their receive their reward in their own souls. At their departure, the governing body has but words of praise and thanks for the Sisters and wishes them God's richest blessings for the future on their hard but beautiful vocation.

Outside the military refuge it was spring; all nature was coming to life. The low sturdy hedge was budding profusely; here and there a cherry tree seemed white with fragrant blossoms. Prematurely, wild roses tried to produce their blooms. An ox-drawn cart lumbered past rudely, nearly forcing the slowly walking Sisters off the road. But Mother did not see. "All around is order and activity," she was thinking. "Everyone and everything belongs to a certain species, and have a particular work to do. And I? What now, O Lord?" No longer an active member of the Servants of the Divine Heart, she felt terribly alone. As for a definite task. Well, it had just been one thing after another, none of them more than temporary.

Father Frederici was waiting for them at the gate of the revamped barracks. *"Grüss Gott,* my Sisters," he hailed them cheerily. "Accept please my deep congratulations for the tremendous job you have done here in Brill." He looked on the downcast women with a heart full of fatherly kindness. "You are unhappy to leave your work here so soon, I know. But, thank you for doing as I requested you. I feel sure that now is the time for work of a different sort on our part. I told you before, on the very day you arrived in Elberfeld that there is much to be done here. We are besieged by the poor; young people come to me with vocations and I cannot help them. And today I received word that smallpox is gaining ground in our region." Mother Odilia stiffened at the mention of the dread disease and immediately began to think of helping.

"No, wait for a moment, Mother," Father Frederici advised. "We must speak first. I have made arrangements for you and Sister here to stay with the Adolph Kreus family. They have a modest cottage on their property in my parish that is standing empty. I am asking you not only to carry on your nursing work in our city now, Mother. Listen carefully. I want you to establish a convent here in Elberfeld, where young ladies can come to devote their life to God and His Works and as sort of auxiliaries to me. We are in such need here," he repeated imploringly.

Mother Odilia realized even while her wise counsellor was speaking that her own anxious question had been answered. She again had a direction in which to work. She agreed quickly to the priest's solemn request. "Indeed, Father. You make me joyful again when truly I was feeling quite desolate. To be allowed to work for Our Lord is all I ask."

"Excellent," rejoiced the old man who sighed deeply to himself as he watched the two sisters disappear down the road on their way to the smallpox victims.

Their organized work of charity and religious rule had met warm approval from the people of the surrounding towns. Soon after Mother Odilia had applied to Pirmasenz for permission to open a branch house of the Holy Family order of the Franciscan rule, she learned that her first religious home was undergoing even worse trials and was on the verge of complete dissolution. She was advised in the ecclesiastical tract from Bavaria to found a new order based, perhaps, on the Third Order Regulars of St. Francis, as the original one had been. Going to Father Frederici with this news, she explained that she was anxious to do his bidding and with the experience of both Pirmasenz and Paris behind, she felt such a thing would be possible.

The cleric paused to consider the current civil strife in all of Germany at that time and the ugly anti-Catholic exhibitions that he had seen repeatedly of late. "Frankly, Mother, I am not sure of our chances to succeed. The people here are unaccustomed to having black-robed women move among them on the streets. There has not been a loss of a young girl or boy, for that matter, to enter a life of religion for generations. And it will not be easy for the people to forget their rancor toward us Catholics which the government has fostered. But as for at least trying, why we have no choice, do we?" The two who had come to understand each other's temperament and perspectives nodded benignly.

Their agreement gave Mother the authority to organize a community life for women who wished to live under the triple vows of poverty, obedience and chastity, and still extend their vocations into the world in which they lived. It was a grand thing for Mother Odilia, separated for over a decade from the replenishing routine. During the days when she stole time from the sick of the town to lay the foundation for her Community, Father Frederici contacted a woman to whom he had already spoken concerning a religious vocation. At the same time, two older women who had observed Mother Odilia's and Sister Magdalene's self-sacrificing lives, their reserve and decorum, came to the Kreus' cottage to offer their aid to the Sisters. They wished, they said, to be a part of the Congregation.

The summer of 1872 found Mother Odilia with a Community of three new Sisters who had completed a year of preparation before being accepted into the Servantes of the Sacred Heart. She had shaped her order in the mold of the ill-fated community to which she had attached herself in Paris. Due to financial circumstances and the pressure of the *kulturkampf,* the Community continued to wear the same habit Mother had donned in Pirmasenz. Their constitution was written by their foundress with the aid of her priest friend. Precarious as their venture was, Mother Odilia had a clear head and knew just what she was trying to do. "If God wills," she would always add.

To the three she gave the names of Sister Francis (Reuter), who was already a trained nurse, Sister Elizabeth (Becker), and Sister Marianna (Herker). The latter was 53, older than Mother herself; she welcomed the day of investiture with immense relief. She was not yet sure of herself in this convent life, but she made every effort to measure up to Mother's standards. Mother had impetuously accepted her with the other two candidates, all of the working class, because she felt that since this work she was doing was not of her own design but God's, God Himself must be sending these particular women to the new little community. In addition, Mother's ability to lead and organize, already so aptly used, led her to feel that she could turn anyone with the proper desire into a good nun. As for the financial problems facing the Congregation she relied on her experience as a mendicant for the Holy Family sisters. She proudly asked for help from whomever she met and willingly distributed her help in return wherever it was needed, as an example to her Congregation.

But daily her trials were growing worse. The conflict between the Roman Catholic Church and the government of the former German states, ruled by William I and led by Count von

Bismarck, which had emerged from the war triumphantly united as the German Empire, was growing. Bismarck was determined that all private educational and ecclesiastical appointments should fall totally under his control. It was commonly agreed by the Catholic hierarchy in Germany that, if this continued, the existing religious orders were in grave danger. Mother knew that a civil law abolishing community life had been drafted and its proclamation was imminent. She daily grew more harassed.

One morning later that summer she and Sister Magdalene were in the garden of the convent rolling bandages with the newly-arrived postulant, Margaret Schneider. Margaret was not yet twenty, but had come from a family of several children. Her father was a tradesman of industrial materials in Elberfeld. She had come to know Mother Odilia and the work of the band of sisters through friends of her family, Gustave and Helena Wegman, who had been cared for by Mother during the epidemic some months before.

The talk was of the strife in the city. "People are becoming openly hostile," said Sister Magdalene, who was curious as to what Mother's thoughts were on the present siege. "I am almost to the point where I dread going out into the city."

"But we can't stop doing that, can we, good Sister?" asked the young Margaret innocently. "What would we do for food?"

Sister Elizabeth, who had been giving instructions to young children of the town in the rectory of St. Joseph's church, came into the shaded yard. She sat down quietly beside her Superior and spoke reverently. "Our Reverend Father has asked me to give you this message, Reverend Mother. He said to tell you that he learned this morning that His Grace, Archbishop Darboy, your friend and his, was executed by the Communards in La Roquette prison over a year ago. He said also to ask us all to pray."

Mother Odilia did not move except to close her eyes slowly. She did not speak, for she was deeply moved by the news brought her from Father Frederici. She was also alarmed by the now open fear shown by her Sisters. She felt her mother's natural desires to protect the small group who had entrusted themselves to her care. Leaving them, she went to her small room to resolve this problem that had been mounting in her and outside of her with each passing

57

day. She knew some drastic decision had to be made. "And we are hardly settled in our new home," she moaned. With the rise of the religious oppression, many Germans had fled to America, she knew. Could they also? The thought had fastened itself in her mind months ago. Now that it still persisted, she decided to at least make a first effort in its direction.

She went to her table and began to compose as forthright a letter as possible to the only personal acquaintances she had in the United States, the Wegmans. With characteristic foresight she had copied their new address in her Mass book. St. Louis, Missouri, U.S.A. It seemed to her a monstrous dream and at the same time a completely logical thing to do. It meant, she knew, that her work here had failed. "But," she told herself, "I have grown accustomed to failure."

> Elberfeld, Germany
> August 11, 1872
>
> Dear Mr. Wegman,
> The present state of affairs with regard to religious, and convents especially, is so discouraging, that we feel inclined to cross the ocean also. Therefore, I would ask you to try to make the acquaintance of some priests, Jesuits or Franciscans, if possible, and inquire of them whether or not it would be advisable for five sisters who devote themselves to the care of the sick to come to America. We do not want to travel without knowing our destination and therefore would ask the advise of some religious authorities to whose guidance we would gladly submit, without, however, expecting any material aid from them.
>
> (Signed) Mother Mary Odilia

Several weeks later the beleaguered Superior found herself joyously composing a second letter to Herr Wegman in America.

> Elberfeld, Germany
> October 2, 1872
>
> Dear Mr. Wegman,
> Twelve days have elapsed since we have received your letter. We cannot express to you our emotions upon reading it; we can only say that no one read it without tears.

First of all, accept our heartfelt thanks for the trouble and care you have taken upon yourself in our behalf. God alone can adequately reward you generously.

After reading the letter, I, of course, went immediately to our Reverend Pastor to obtain his advice on so serious a matter. Our Pastor regrets our departure from Elberfeld because we had rented a larger house last May and have extended our activities with the aid of more sisters. Nevertheless, he thinks we will do well to go to America, for it is impossible, under present conditions, to re-establish a community in Germany. We would rather cross all the seas than give up our vocations and return to the world.

After making a novena, notice of removal was given and we are selling our furniture. We have decided, with the help of God, to leave Elberfeld on the sixteenth of this month; on the eighteenth, we will board a steamer at Hamburg and, please God, will reach St. Louis on the Feast of All Saints.

Now our ardent prayer to the Sacred Hearts of Jesus and Mary and good St. Joseph is that we may find a small home and our vocation. We are full of confidence and courage.

May we ask you to look for two small rooms where rent is cheap and, if possible, near a Catholic Church. We will and must content ourselves with the bare necessities and must limit our expenses to the utmost.

All, all for Jesus! How happy we shall be to meet you again, and together we will praise the goodness of God toward us.

Mother Odilia laid down the long black quill with a smile of satisfaction. Triumphantly, she sealed the letter and carried it herself to the tiny post office.

"Now," she said aloud, "we can begin all over again."

CHAPTER SIX

She Hath Put Her Hand
to Strong Things

T HE band of six German women, marked by their dress as withdrawn from the world and by their sweet simplicity as holy nuns, made the trans-Atlantic trip on the steamship Allemania, owned by the Hamburg-American Line. The crossing was a treacherous one, and Mother Odilia spent most of the trip tirelessly caring for her seasick sisters as well as many other suffering passengers. Her able nurse, Sister Francis, became seriously ill during the long trip. Fearing they would lose her before their new work had even begun, the Servants prayed fervently.

Her first glimpse of the New York City harbor for Mother Odilia seemed to flip back the years. The mighty Statue of Liberty standing regally to greet the immigrants was for her the beloved Statue of Bavaria in the Theresienwiesen which had so moved her in her youth. She spent the final hours of the three weeks afloat contemplating the similarity of the two inanimate women and came to the conclusion that this new land's sign of justice was the most appropriate welcome America could have extended to her and her refugee band. It encouraged her to look to the future; to forget the hardships of the past.

As they disembarked, the Sisters found, as they had prepared themselves to find, that their new country was a glorious, confusing land. Most of the Sisters had learned enough English to get

61

by. Mother, mindful of the frugality of her purse and the still long journey ahead, led her companions to the railway station.

In spite of her stout heart, she felt a strange fear creep over her. Not for herself only, but for the other five who had left their families and homeland; for the loyal Sister Magdalene, for the frail Sister Francis, for jolly Sister Elizabeth, for Sister Marianna who would have a difficult time learning the English language at her advanced age and, not the least, for the high-spirited postulant Margaret. What if having brought them so far? . . . Then, hastily, she prayed, "Please, God, forgive me for doubting. I place all my trust in You."

Together the weary group recited their rosary beads, as the noisy train carried them to their destination, the gas-lit city of St. Louis, halfway across the vast new country. They used the five day trip partly to rest, for they were weary and discouraged. The five-dollar gold piece Mother had brought from Elberfeld for food on the journey was quickly used up; twice they were forced to stop along the way to beg for more money.

Mr. Wegman was at Union Station as the train pulled in that cold November 16, 1872, exactly one month after their departure from Elberfeld. Greeting them cordially, their old friend took the Sisters immediately to the residence of Reverend Henry Muehl-siepen, Vicar General of the St. Louis archdiocese, whose warm welcome made them forget for the time being at least, their hunger and fatigue. Most Reverend Peter Richard Kendrick, who was Archbshop of St. Louis at the time, sent best wishes and his blessing. Mother Odilia was overcome with joy at this reception for her community.

After introducing her Sisters to the good Father, she presented him with a letter from their former spiritual director in Elberfeld:

> The religious of the Third Order of St. Francis, Sister Mary Odilia Berger and Sister Mary Magdalene Fuerst, who formerly lived in Paris but who were compelled on account of their German nativity to leave France two years ago, have since then lived here. During the Franco-Prussian war, they were in charge of the military hospital here in Elberfeld.

By their untiring labors and their skillful treatment of the sick and wounded soldiers, they merited the grateful acknowledgement of the soldiers and also of the officials.

When their services were no longer required they nursed the sick in the homes. Here, too, they proved themselves discreet and indefatigable nurses, especially during the smallpox epidemic which raged here at the time.

By their sacrificing labors and by their Christian and religious deportment, they have won the general esteem of my parish.

(Signed) Frederici, Pastor
Elberfeld, 12 October, 1872

Reverend Muehlsiepen was obviously impressed as he folded the letter.

Father Faerber, who was to be their spiritual director, took them to temporary living quarters with the Ursuline nuns.

As soon as this new protector had announced that the Ursuline sisters were to be their benefactors, Mother grew excited despite her extreme fatigue. Could this be a mere coincidence, she wondered, that now in America the Ursulines should be offering them a first home just as they had been the first teachers in her childhood long ago in Bavaria? It was insignificant, of course, she told herself. Nevertheless, her arrival with her band of four professed Sisters and the young postulant, Margaret, at the stately convent, solid-looking and secure, was like a homecoming. "I feel as though I am returning to old friends," she spoke to the enthusiastic Sisters who welcomed them.

They had their first cooked meal since they had left Elberfeld. "Bless us O Lord," they joined in the new prayer, "and these Thy gifts which we are about to receive from Thy bounty." "From Thy bounty," mother repeated in her thoughts as the many sisters became acquainted over their meals. "Yes, we are just beggars like our holy Father St. Francis, living on the bounty of God."

For the first month following their coming to the Midwest the Servants of the Sacred Heart helped their hostesses with house work and sewing, mainly recouping their strength after the exhausting months of preparation and travel. Their scanty funds and unsettling sea voyage had left each of the Sisters, and Sister Francis especially, undernourished physically and spiritually. Their very presence within an established convent, despite the fact that it was not their own, brought pleasure unbounded. The Ursuline house in St. Louis had, even at that time, been granted the special privilege of having the Blessed Sacrament always ensconced in its beautiful chapel. This living in God's house, in the truest sense, was a unique experience for the immigrant nuns. Even Mother Odilia and the faithful Sister Magdalene had not known this exquisite boon as resident nuns in their faltering motherhouse in Pirmasenz. The Ursulines were "established, recognized, permanent. They were permitted to take permanent vows. Spiritual recognition and respectability was theirs," Mother observed.

During that first month Mother often meditated on these things as she knelt in stillness before the Eucharist. "Oh, how I hunger for these holy blessings for my hard-pressed Sisters." She would run to the chapel where her Lover waited and spend full hours there in conversation with Him whenever her schedule allowed. Her great eyes seeing only the vision of the Presence within, she realized simply that although her flair for life and her enjoyment of people still remained, "This is where I am at home. Here where there is no failure, no success, no anger or jealousy or innuendo — only peace."

Her time was consumed in great part with learning all there was to know about the already great, but rapidly expanding, city of St. Louis. The Wegmans were her guides, and they helped her understand her new home, knowing first hand, as they did, the peculiar problems of the German immigrant who speaks but little English.

They showed Mother about the new industrial metropolis, explaining details and English expressions with great patience. It was as a result of these excursions that Mother realized joyfully that the Sisters' flight from persecution had not been one merely of self-preservation. Here in the new world all about her were suffering people and sickness, poverty, and disease. She saw plainly that the business of maintaining her order would go hand in hand with the work of charity to which the half dozen women were so capably and willingly attracted.

She saw, too, that the tremendous transplanting she had anticipated both eagerly and apprehensively was not the complete change she had expected. All around her were familiar sights. She thrilled to see charging down Market street the grand gray horses drawing huge loads of beer just as they had in Regen. Having grown accustomed to the sight of these glorious brewery horses, she felt almost as though she had not left her own country. "Why those horses are like ambassadors of labor from across the ocean," she exclaimed interrupting Gustave Wegman, as they walked. "I have always loved the sight of their haunch muscles rippling under hide that is as lustrous as a general's boot. And the perfection of the way they work together!" she marvelled.

"Yes, Mother, I know how you feel," he agreed. "You see St. Louis makes a lot of beer, just like in our old country, eh? And you know what else? It is filled with German and Bavarian people, too. Why there are some parts of the city where our language is more popular than the English. So you will not be too much troubled by a 'language barrier,' as they say here. More and more of our people are coming here so fast that the city will probably be twice as big in ten years. St. Louis has industry for us, railroads. It is a lot like home, ya? But," he continued in a changed tone, "there is something here we could not find in our homeland. Here we can be what we want to be. The European fetters are gone here. St. Louis especially gives a man a chance to work and better himself, no matter what his beginnings may be. St. Louis is growing and we foreigners can grow right with it. We can even grow to be Americans," he ended with excited waving of his hand.

Mother was delighted to see that her new city was also laid out on a grand river, the Mississippi, just like Regen and Paris were. In time she would grow to love the river and see in it the means whereby St. Louis nourished the regions to the south and west, a parallel with the work she meant to do here.

One morning coming up from the cold, damp basement where she had been helping with the washing, Mother Odilia walked firmly to the Ursuline superior's office with a startling announcement. "We will be moving next week, Mother," she said matter-of-factly. "You will never know how much your hospitality has meant to us. We ask God to reward you for your kindness."

"Why, you have been with us only a few weeks. Must you leave already?" Mother Aloysia, the superior, exclaimed.

"*Ya*, it is better for us to find a house of our own," she explained haltingly, her inborn independence exerting itself.

"There will be much we can do to help you get started in your new home, my dear. Please let us help," Mother Aloysia graciously requested.

With the combined assistance of their generous friends, the Wegmans, and their spiritual director, the little order found a new home, thus solving their most pressing problem. Father Faerber was pastor of St. Mary's church, situated on Third and Gratiot streets in downtown St. Louis. Through his intercession, the Sisters were given, at no cost, the upper story of a poor frame house a block from St. Mary's church. The rooms had gone unused for many months, so were dirty and in bad repair. The valiant Sisters, courted still by an ever-present poverty, had scarcely dropped their bundles after walking the distance from the Ursuline home to their new one in the bitter December cold, when they began planning how they would scrub, plaster, and give respectability to the flat.

Mother was triumphant in her reserved way. "See, Sisters, a kitchen here for cooking and eating. It will be big enough, don't you think? And two rooms besides where we can do our work. And the attic is large enough for our six beds. We could not hope for more." She scurried from doorway to doorway showing up the advantages of the new home to each of the nuns in a childlike way.

"And, besides," she continued, "we are so very near St. Mary's Church. Look, there it is, you can see it even from here." She wiped the grime from the narrow window so the others crowding around her could get a better view.

In spite of their generous hearts, everyone was thinking the same thing, but it was Postulant Margaret who revealed her thoughts.

"But, Mother," she said, "the rooms are almost bare. . . ."

"Don't worry, Margaret," Mother replied in her quiet way. "Let's get on with our work. God will see to it that we get some furniture."

"Mother could be exasperatingly optimistic," the young woman felt humbly. But in this, as in all other events in their lives, our Lord seemed to say, "Ask and it shall be given unto you." From various sources the furniture came quickly until the drab rooms took on the appearance of a home. Six low iron beds had been donated by their Ursuline friends for the icy attic, before the plastered walls had dried. A table, big enough for all of them and six odd chairs came from Father Faerber. In the kitchen the squat sooty stove, also a gift of the Ursulines, devoured wood to keep Mother Odilia's band comfortable.

Within a few days of their arrival on Gratiot street came Christmas. Mother Odilia had planned for the happy feast, her favorite, to be a climax to the laborious work of the Sisters in making the miserable house into a satisfactory home. The day before she had gone out on a mysterious mission. On her arm hung a good-sized wicker basket she had discovered abandoned in the new flat. The basket was open but deep and sturdy. It was to survive her memorable journeys, during which great quantities of medicine and money were dropped in it, to be revered long after Mother's death as a relic of her charity. Mother was searching for gifts of flour with which to prepare pancakes for frying on the temperamental stove as a special breakfast treat and for some crib figures, to recreate the Christmas scene. As she walked gingerly toward the center of St. Louis, a woman stopped her. "Pardon me, I am Molly Brieghaus," the jolly-faced woman began. "You are the leader of the new Sisters in our parish, aren't you?" Mother nodded and smiled openly. "Well," the older woman went on, "I've been noticing that your house up there is never lit up after dark and me and my neighbors wondered if maybe you didn't have lights."

Mother was unsure what the woman meant. She opened her eyes a little wider and set her jaw as she nodded her head just slightly. "Ah, then, I have more than enough for my little place," the stranger said a little embarrassed. "Could I bring one of my lamps over with some coal oil for you?" Mother's smile was brilliant. "Why, how kind of you, Mrs. Brieghaus. And just now I was searching for something I could give my poor Sisters as a Christmas gift. You have solved my problem. How can I thank you?" She walked on, warmed by the encounter and by the realization that somehow the vision of people around her was constantly being broadened to encompass and fulfill the needs of her Community. "Now we can begin to sew some new habits and do some spiritual reading in our evenings," she thought.

Like the wicker basket the gift lamp would remain to be treasured by Mother's daughters, descendants of her spirit, in the Motherhouse museum. Many of the lighting fixtures in the convent itself would be designed to further commemorate the incident.

Late that afternoon, Mother was busy in the new convent disguising rescued boxes from the moving debris for the makeshift crèsche and for an altar on which to perch the much-traveled statue of St. Joseph, which still stood protectively over Mother Odilia's work. Her work done, she stood back to survey the work room which she had enriched by her love and labor. "Our first Christmas in America," she mused.

The wind outside was screaming; snow had been blown into deep drifts outside the Sisters' modest home. At their work the assembled community wore cloaks and rubbed their hands to fight off the cold. The holiday season was just ending for the work-weary housekeepers when Sister Elizabeth returned from a food-begging trip in a frantic state.

"Oh, Mother Odilia, I have bad news," she moaned. "There are three cases of smallpox on Gratiot Street and people say it is spreading and maybe there will be an epidemic." Sister Elizabeth was breathless. Mother Odilia, who had risen to accept the information replied, "May it please God, we can aid these poor sufferers. It seems we have just come in time." Almost immediately Father Faerber came in with more information about the suffering in the stricken homes. He and Mother Odilia consulted as how best to begin their public work in this emergency. "Thank God, you are here to help these miserable people, Mother," he murmured. "I can't tell you what a relief it is to me to know there will be aid and comfort for these poor people. Before, when the scare came, they were left to die mercilessly. Truly, you come like a merchant ship full of love and charity directly from God."

"My beloved Sisters, our work here in our new home is beginning," Mother later told her band. "You are all familiar with smallpox. I do want to remind you before we are pushed into the fury of work and are too busy to be together that our primary object is to strive earnestly for our own spiritual perfection according to our vows. Each of you has chosen to do this in caring for the sick, especially the poor. True, we have in the old days been able to open orphanages and homes for working girls. You all know my hopes for our order. But now we must do only what we are able to do, and to do that as perfectly as we can."

Each of the Sisters was selflessly eager to go to the sick anywhere she was needed. Mother assigned them to help as many as possible. Postulant Margaret, as well as two new candidates who had already come to swell their ranks, were each to accompany one of the Sisters.

Those were strenuous days for the heroic Mother and her Sisters who had already undergone so many hardships. Now the two room convent was always empty during the day and sometimes even through the night. The key was left in a designated place so that whoever returned first might search the impoverished pantry for something to satisfy the gnawings of hunger of the few who could return.

Mother Odilia acted as a commuter between her Sisters and their charges. When she herself was not engaged in nursing a particular family, she would relieve one of her Sisters to enable them to get a little rest. Any hour of the day or night she might be seen, her basket on her arm, going from house to house dispensing nourishment to her Sisters or bedding, food, and medications to patients. The vitality of the intrepid woman was not such as comes from good food, or any such physical stimulant. Her dynamic energy stemmed from only one source, her love of God!

So devotedly did the Sisters nurse these victims of the dread plague that they became intimately associated with the disease. They were known as the "smallpox Sisters." The postulants, new to the distasteful work of caring for the dying in great numbers, suffered with humiliation when people crossed the street as they approached. They were as outcasts who fully realized the joy of being outcasts for Christ.

The Sisters carried little bells, which they rang as anyone approached to caution them against contact with smallpox.

Mother Odilia was determined that the Sisters' spiritual life keep pace with their material activities. Now as the winter of 1873 melted into spring, the great day for which her three postulants had been longing arrived. It was the day of their investiture. They had made a fervent retreat, spending whatever free time they had in the uncommodious attic. It was Mother's wish that the retreatants be thus separated from the rest of the Community to further their opportunities for recollection and prayer.

Mother Odilia knew full well that, under normal circumstances, the life of the postulant was a well-organized, rather regimented thing. During the first six months, a candidate must spend her time adjusting to convent life and her associates and learning the fundamentals of obedience and spiritual detachment. Her day must begin and end with meditation and include housework and studies of theology, of the religious life, and care of the sick. After the first half of her first year was ended, the postulant would usually begin her novitiate which, after concentrated study and prayer, would be climaxed by her profession. "But ours are not normal times," she maintained as she beat down the longing in her heart for a peaceful routine for her charges. "My dear postulants have

Four pioneers: Mother Mary Odilia (seated center), Sister Mary Magdalene, Sister Mary Elizabeth, and Sister Mary Francis.

Right Reverend Monsignor Henry Muehl-siepen, Vicar General of the St. Louis arch-diocese in 1872.

Reverend Father William Faerber. The kind pastor of St. Mary's Church, St. Louis, who became the Sisters spiritual director on their arrival in America, November 16, 1872.

The straw basket in which Mother Odilia carried the donations of food, medicine, and money to her Sisters and patients. The basket is preserved in the museum at the Motherhouse.

The second story and attic of this house within the shadow of St. Mary's Church became "home" to Mother Odilia and her first Sisters shortly after they arrived in St. Louis.

The coal oil lamp given to Mother Odilia by a neighbor to light the Sisters' first home in St. Louis. The lamp is in the museum at the Mother-house.

been asked to do the hardest things first. They have been put to the tests of perfect obedience to my every order, of humility on the streets, of the deepest love in giving themselves to the care of these smallpox and cholera victims.

"I must accept this as the dear Postulants and Sisters have accepted it," she chided herself. "The time for prayer lies in the future." She hesitated for a moment as she was forming the thought, then the veil fell away. "What a *dompkoff* I am! Our whole life is a prayer just as we live it now," she marvelled.

It was March 19th, the feast of St. Joseph. Mother proudly watched in St. Mary's church as the solemn young women received their black wool habits, which they had made themselves, from the hands of Father Faerber at St. Joseph's altar. Father Faerber exhorted them with Christ's own words, "Take up your cross daily and follow Me." Then the three postulants made their promise to live as Franciscans, having already tasted the bitterness of their words in their errands of mercy.

The two native American candidates, Rosalia Lippke and Mary Kalthof took the names Sister Theresa and Sister Josepha, respectively. Margaret was to be known in religion as Sister Mary Odilia, as she had requested out of respect and love for her spiritual mother.

That spring three new candidates arrived to join the courageous Sisters who were assuaging the afflicted city. Mother's joy was tempered by the decision of Sister Marianne, who was now approaching sixty, to return to her native Rhineland. She was too old, she told Mother sadly, to learn this difficult language and much as she loved to work among the sick, she felt unsettled and unhappy in America. She expressed especially her gratitude to Mother for working so hard to train her to be a true religious.

Mother Odilia, too, was worried. "Our family is increasing and to ask eleven Sisters to be content in this small house is not good," she told herself. So, she wrote, as she had done since girlhood, a letter to St. Joseph:

My dearest Father St. Joseph,

A million times I greet thee through the Sweet Heart of Jesus thy Son. Thou knowest that I have already asked thy foster Son to increase thy honor and glory. To behold thee in most sublime glory would be part of my eternal felicity.

To you, I entrust this house with all its debts and all the Sisters in the house of thy spouse, our dearest Mother. You know we need more room; build therefore, just as it pleases you; it is your business; we are instruments in your hands. Help us on the way of perfection and make use of us for the greater honor and glory of the Sacred Hearts of Jesus and Mary.

You alone can and must establish and conserve this community. Obtain the grace of perseverance for all those whom thou hast brought here and send us many more during the year. Thou art so good and powerful, that I will set no limits to the number. Last year, you sent one more than I asked for.

O ever be a Father to us, is our daily prayer. Teach us to serve the Sacred Heart faithfully after thy example and help us to become worthy of the name of thy spouse.

My dearest Father, casting myself in spirit at thy feet, I remain,

Your ever loving child,
Mother Odilia

Leaving the Sisters' room, she was startled to hear: "Mother, what shall we do?" It was Sister Magdalene's voice.

"Why, Sister, what is the trouble?"

"There is a bum, I mean a beggar, at our door. He's asking for food and all we have in the house is one loaf of bread, and the Sisters are coming home now tired and . . ."

But Mother interrupted the excited Sister, "Let us give the poor man what he asks for, Sister; the Lord will provide for us."

Sister Magdalene opened her mouth to protest but thought better of it. Instead, she watched while Mother Odilia herself took the precious loaf to the shabby mendicant.

Barely one hour later, as Sister Magdalene was still fretting over the prospect of no bread for the returning Sisters, a knock came at the door. A child, whom they had not seen before, stood holding out a pan of huge golden-brown, freshly baked rolls in her hands, which she held up to the Sister, who stared in speechless amazement.

"Mother sent them," was all the girl said, then ran down the path to the street.

"The Lord has come; you are the Lord today, little one," called the humble Superior after the flying figure.

CHAPTER SEVEN

Many Daughters Have Gathered Together

MOTHER's bold bid for a new home for her expanding order was in keeping with her character. She was convinced that God's
will for her was to lead these women He was sending her on to
greater and greater works of charity which, her common sense told
her, would exist till the end of time. So, undaunted by lack of
funds and overwork, she determined to do what must be done for
her Community's well-being.

Early in the summer of this same year, 1873, Mother requested from the chancellery of St. Louis some sort of aid to carry
out her plan. The ecclesiastical authorities granted her permission
to erect a convent on a vacant lot directly south of St. Mary's
Church, on ground belonging to Father Faerber's church. The Sisters would have to raise the money to pay for it themselves, however.

Mother made arrangements for the work to begin, consulting
first with Father Faerber, then with architects and a builder.
Through her months of labor in the city she had found a rewarding
group of willing benefactors, among them both religious and lay
people from the highest to the lowest levels of life. From each
she asked help only to do God's work; help in the form of money
and materials came miraculously. Convinced of the soundness of
her purpose, Mother commissioned the building of the new convent even before enough money for a first payment had been col-

lected. Then throughout the summer she spent all her free time begging alms.

On a breezy, exhilarating day when the intense summer heat of St. Louis was waning, Mother Odilia led her Sisters on their second full-scale migration, this time only half-way down the block. "How different this move is from the last," commented Sister Magdalene, as the Sisters made ready to leave their second floor refuge. "It is truly the Providence of God," replied Mother happily.

There was much excitement in the air as Sisters scurried up and down stairs, back and forth between houses. Sisters Josepha and Elizabeth helped the generous Karl Kneff, their fruit vendor who had offered his services and his wagon to the nuns for their move. Together they dragged the furniture down the steep tenement stairs. Madonna and Lena, the new candidates, were given the privilege of carrying the venerated statue of St. Joseph from its packing case to a new pedestal. Mother had arranged for St. Joseph's image to be enshrined in the small convent chapel. In future days it would be even further esteemed by her descendants who would place it in one of the niches below the impressive statues of Our Lady of Lourdes in her shrine on the south end of the present convent garden. The statue now stands on an altar of porous stone on the front of which is inlaid a large square bearing a round seal with a heart in the center. Around the outside in a circle is the inscription "Semper Laudetur Divinissimum Cor Jesu" (Praised be the most divine Heart of Jesus forever) and the date, 1873. This stone originally was above the first Motherhouse of the Sisters of St. Mary on Third and Gratiot Streets.

It is said that St. Joseph feels quite at home with the Sisters, for into his opened hand many a note petitioning one thing or another is slipped. Witnesses attest to the fact that he is just as prodigious with these present day daughters of St. Francis as he was with their Mother, Odilia.

The three-story structure resounded with exlamations of delight as the Sisters waged an exploration. On the first floor they went to the tiny chapel to murmur a thanksgiving. Then they examined the sewing room with its two large windows, the spacious reception room with its straight-backed chairs, round mahogany table on the center of which stood a very shiny brass oil lamp, all donated by kind benefactors. Mother led the way to the second floor with her excited Sisters close behind her.

"Oh," exclaimed the breathless Postulant Rosie, pointing to the room ahead, which proudly displayed four long tables with fifteen matching chairs.

"Look, there is even a reformatory."

Peels of laughter shook the room as Sister Elizabeth, who had charge of candidates, corrected her. "Refectory, Rosie; not reformatory."

On the same floor was a large community room and even an infirmary.

"Now we can get sick," Postulant Lena sighed, as if just the prospect of lying in one of the two white beds with smooth grey blankets, was a luxury she had not dared dream of.

Eagerly, the Sisters made their way to still a third floor. Ah, the dormitories! "No more crowded sleeping quarters," they exclaimed. Each Sister could at last have her own little cell and privacy.

Sister Mary Odilia, who had been doing the washing for the group, suddenly realized that a very important feature had, she thought, been neglected.

"Mother," she asked desperately, "what about the washing? Is there a place in the cellar where we can put our tubs and washboard?"

"Oh, no Sister, the laundry is in the attic. Our house is very up-to-date," she teased.

At this, they all trudged up curious to inspect the new laundry: a large bare room with a window facing north and another arranged to catch the first rays of the morning sun. "Of course, it will look more like a laundry when the tubs and buckets have been lugged up from the back porch," Mother apologized.

Laughing, the young Sister lost no time. She planted the metal washboard which she had been carrying under her arm against the south wall and proceeded to run down the three flights of stairs to bring up her other equipment.

"Well, it's all very wonderful," exclaimed the delighted Postulant Madonna, "but, but, is there no place to . . ." She leaned over to whisper to Rosie. Madonna was from an Italian immigrant family and could not speak the English language too well as yet.

"She means," Rosie interpreted, "where is the kitchen?"

"Yes," spoke up Sister Mary solemnly, as if a calamity had befallen, "yes, where is the kitchen?"

The Sisters looked at Mother in questioning silence. No, they hadn't seen a kitchen. But Mother saved them from further grief by a cheerful, "Just follow me." Down the steps they went single file, past the dormitories, refectory, down, down, into the basement. And there stood their own temperamental sooty wood burner to welcome them in the large kitchen.

As if they had not all had enough surprises for one day, Mother again led them upstairs and out into the tiny yard behind the new convent house. In a far corner was a grotto in which a large statue of the Pieta was enshrined. Instinctively they knelt in gratitude to their dear heavenly Mother.

On October 10, 1873, the new convent was blessed and dedicated to God's Mother. It was the eve of the feast of the Maternity of the Blessed Virgin. The Sisters were busy erecting a shrine for their beloved Immaculate Conception image in the parlor, the statue Mother had brought from Germany. It was more than two feet tall, was carved from teakwood and bore a golden cloak over a simple mauve gown. Mary's arms extended beseechingly to the insurgent group of religious; her face wore a listening expression. While they were still working a strange thing happened which altered the course of Mother Odilia's congregation. Father Faerber joined them in the parlor and asked Mother if she would grant him a special favor. The happy Sisters, with Mother in their midst, listened expectantly. "Since, Sisters, we have done an unusual thing here by having your convent share the very wall of our St. Mary's church, and since the people of St. Louis already are calling

St. Mary's Convent adjoining old St. Mary's Church on Third and Gratiot Streets — 1873.

The statue of the Immaculate Conception which Mother Odilia brought with her from Germany and which was later placed in the parlor of the new St. Mary's Convent.

The coat of arms
of the Sisters of St. Mary.

The corporate seal
of the Sisters of St. Mary

The much-traveled statue of St. Joseph which stood protectively over Mother Odilia's work and in whose hand were placed the letters of petition and love she wrote him.

you the Sisters of St. Mary because of your proximity to our church, would you, if I ask it, change your title from Servants of the Sacred Heart to Sisters of St. Mary?" He waited to assay their response. All eyes in the large group were on Mother Odilia, who, realizing that she could not refuse such an earnest request from one who had been so good to her Community, submitted with a smile and a nod knowing that the red cincture which her sisters wore would always be a reminder of their former title.

During the late summer months, the smallpox plague had released its hold on St. Louis but now in the fall it attacked with renewed vigor. This time it brought with it its twin terror, cholera.

So many requests came for the Sisters' help that Mother Odilia did not know how she could meet the demands. Gathering her Sisters in prayer she assigned them to special posts. She herself would go to the home of the good and generous Frederick Baumeier, who had been supplying the Sisters with milk since their coming to St. Louis.

As Mother arrived at the comfortable brownstone home, she found the dying man's wife distraught. Abandoned by all her friends, Mrs. Baumeier turned for strength to a strange woman whom she sensed could sustain her in this grief. Mother comforted the frightened woman as best she could and put her to bed, then set to work. There was so much to be done. Putting on her dark blue apron and rolling up her sleeves, she assembled the needed supplies. A bucket of cool water to bathe the feverish body of her friend and benefactor, many dry blankets, newspaper for the accompanying vomitting and diarrhea.

Mother worked over Baumeier far into the night; as she worked she prayed. She prayed silently and from time to time she prayed aloud into the ear of the delirious victim who threw his great weight from side to side. Now and then his parched lips moved as if to follow her prayers but he made no sound. As she blessed him with the holy water which she always carried in her basket, he finally lay still. Mother Odilia knew the man had died.

79

She stayed until dawn, cleaning the germ-laden house and comforting the widow.

Walking meditatively back to her convent home early that morning, insensible to fatigue and hunger, she was stopped by a frail little woman she did not know. "Mother, please come. My son's family is so sick. It must be cholera. We're the Baker's. It isn't far." Mother squeezed her arm reassuringly and said she would come within an hour. She never refused any requests of God's sick poor! She intended to go to the Baker's as soon as she could check on all her Sisters, but on arriving home, she met young Sister Theresa who adamantly refused to let her go.

"No, Mother," she pleaded, "I am young and strong. Please let me go. You are so worn out. You must rest today."

Sister Theresa's entreaties won out. She found, as she later reported to Mother, that the entire family, the parents and the two small boys, were in the advanced stages of cholera. Their miserable home was a one-room shack. A wealthy lady she met on the way had promised to send supplies to Sister Theresa, but, unfortunately, either through forgetfulness on her part or through fear of contagion on the part of the one commissioned by her, nothing came. The scanty provisions that were in the house had to be reserved for the patients; consequently, Sister went for two days and nights without anything to eat or drink. On the second day of her fast, she went to the public well to get some fresh water in an empty tomato can. Looking down the street, she saw Mother Odilia and another Sister coming along the Iron Mountain track nearby. In those days, the Sisters were obliged to walk because the public knew they were caring for the infected patients and feared coming in contact with them on the horse-drawn streetcars.

Seeing the Sisters coming toward her, Sister Theresa went back into the shack thinking they were coming to bring her provisions. After a long time she realized with a shrinking heart that they must have passed by. Had Mother Odilia forgotten her child?

That night in a dream our Lady appeared to Mother Odilia and told her that Sister Theresa was in need of food and other supplies. Rising immediately though it was scarcely dawn and she had had but three hours sleep Mother walked rapidly to the Baker house with provisions for her heroic Sister.

Although Mother Odilia saw that the constant demands for caring for the sick in their homes were not lessening, she decided to send another shoot of religious activity into a neglected field. As in Paris where she had gone to do primarily this type of charity, Mother felt obliged to provide a solution to the pressing need of unfortunate young unwed mothers-to-be who needed not only a home, but nursing care as well. With the guidance and financial aid of men of ability and integrity who stood ready to help her, Mother purchased a small house in the extreme northern part of St. Louis called College Hill, in a section known as "Lowell." Details of the site were not completely satisfactory, such as the only source of water being a well quite far from the house and the size of the house itself, but Mother felt that time was pressing. She was determined to have the home ready before winter brought further suffering to the tormented women. So, soon after the glorious ceremonies of the dedication of the new convent on Third and Gratiot streets, Mother and Father Faerber less ceremoniously welcomed their first guests to their temporary home. Christmas was about to surmount the sadness of Advent. Mother was moved to call the new endeavor "La Crêsche."

Still another call to activity was to come to Mother Odilia's already burdened corps late in 1873. While aiding in the settling of the first group of young women at the Lowell house Mother was presented with a message from Father William Koch of St. Peter's parish at St. Charles, Missouri.

"Your reputation as Smallpox Sisters has reached me here in St. Charles," the letter explained. "We have been stricken down by the epidemic without warning and cannot survive without help. Mother Odilia, come to us with your knowledge of how to combat this awful thing. Please, do not refuse."

81

Mother was taken aback as she read the missive. The new home here had seemed a heavy enough tax to put on her Sisters. How could she ask them now to leave the convent for a strange place of misery nearly twenty miles away? She was deeply concerned for what sacrifices this would mean for those who might go.

Hope ran high in the budding congregation for a release of the scourge in the Midwestern region. Yet, the days raced by almost unnoticed by the ever-toiling Sisters, and the epidemic raged fiercely. As new circles of the populace fell under the highly-contagious breathing poison, the Sisters made more and more demands upon themselves. Rarely was the community life able to be maintained. Besides all her other crosses, Mother was further burdened by the personal responsibility she felt for the well-being of her Sisters, physical as well as spiritual. She especially stressed to each of her Sisters that the decision to go among these highly infectious diseases rested with them alone. She would request them to work among the smallpox and cholera but she could not order them. The possibility of seeing one of these innocents fall prey to the epidemic haunted her ceaselessly. But she was equally moved by the glorious spectacle of the human angels with no apparent hesitation going into situations certain to bring them sickness and death for the "glory of God" as was their intention. Miraculously, thus far, all the Sisters had been spared.

All were visibly saddened as Sister Elizabeth, who had come with Mother from Elberfeld, took two of the new Sisters and as veritable missionaries left St. Mary's on the horse drawn wagon. Mother had given the three admirable Sisters all the funds and supplies she could. She counselled them to keep in touch. "My heart and prayers will be with you, my dear Sisters," she spoke to them in farewell. "Remember that with this new cross God is always with you to help you carry it." Her words were characteristically simple and sound, and the departing Sisters understood and felt well prepared for their work. In St. Charles, they worked under the guidance of the pastor of St. Peter's and were housed in small quarters on Jackson street. They went out each day nursing the stricken in their homes during the two-year siege that smallpox held on the city.

In answer to the daily prayers of the desperately concerned Mother Odilia, the protecting hand of God shielded the three diligent workers who, although they daily came in the closest possible contact with the disease, returned home still in good health.

Work was a way of life for the Sisters as the anniversary of their arrival in America came and went. Mother Odilia, whose selfless activity and holiness constantly beckoned her Community of fifteen Sisters and three Postulants on to greater sacrifices, strived to manage their affairs. At the Lowell home, which was developing well despite a shortage of workers, the young women themselves, Mother discovered, were anxious to help the dedicated religious. Despite utter poverty, the Motherhouse was full of joy and accomplishment. Three new Professions had been made which added to Mother's fold: Sisters Clara Harbers, Agnes Hellmeyer and Ludovica Hoef.

Ordinarily, breakfast for all of them consisted of dry bread and "coffee" made of dried peas, but occasionally they would have jam on their bread, this delicacy being a donation from the market.

It was customary for the Sisters to visit Union market several times a week. Two of them, taking a large wash basket, would make the rounds of the stalls, begging for potatoes, vegetables or anything that the charity of the vendors prompted them to give. When the basket was full, they would carry it home and then come back with another empty one. Very often, it is true, they were given only such produce as could not be sold: the frost bitten apples, shrunken turnips, woody radishes, over-ripe tomatoes. But parts of them were edible, and the Sisters were grateful for each small blessing.

Trudging wearily homeward one evening, Sister Mary Agnes and Sister Mary Ludovica were indulging in the luxurious prospect of an evening at home. It had been so long since either of them had been at the convent for any length of time. In fact, the new community room in which they anticipated an hour of recreation now and then had seldom been used since they moved there. For the most part the house was empty. Mother and the Sisters were out all of the day and usually even at night.

"Tonight," sighed the tired Sister Agnes, "I'm going to try out one of those new chairs. I haven't even sat in one of them yet."

They were finishing their recitation of the rosary when they arrived. Mother Odilia was standing at the door waiting for them. Addressing Sister Agnes she asked gently, "Sister, can you go on a sick call? A Mr. Mueller came here to say his wife and all his children have the smallpox and he cannot get anyone to care for them."

Sister Agnes' tiredness fell away before her generous spirit as she replied, "Gladly, Mother."

Where had she heard that name before? No, this was not a poor family; one could tell that by the address. The nun was puzzled as she hurried down the street.

Entering the house, she caught sight of Mr. Mueller. Their eyes met and then she remembered! Two days before, she had come to this very house on a begging trip and this same man had driven her away telling her that she should work for her money and not expect to lead an idle life and then live off other people.

Sister wondered for a scant moment if the harassed father, caught up in his own harshness, recognized her or at least her habit? Taking command of the hysterical household, she suggested Mueller himself remain away from the west wing of the estate where all the sick were gathered. Her work was to be well rewarded this time, for as she went about busily from one to another of the Mueller family, Sister could see that the attack was a slight one. The medicine she had to offer took quick effect. Under her devoted care were Mrs. Mueller, three Mueller children, the youngest of which was only four months old, and Mrs. Mueller's aged mother. Within two weeks the Sisters of St. Mary were no longer needed by the Muellers. Sister gathered her bag and cloak and left without exchanging words with the relieved master of the house.

The routine of work and privation for the Sisters was punctuated by laughter and lightheartedness, which might be hard for anyone familiar with the unrelenting dark times to comprehend. The Sisters were intensely devoted and sensitive to Mother's leadership and wisdom. Perhaps it was because Mother herself was always the first to answer some new demand for food or care before she called on her daughters to do so; perhaps it was purely due to an appreciation of her simplicity and integrity. They each used her example as a measure of their own spiritual life. Some of the Sisters' happiest memories of the early community life were of the informal gatherings around their great table on those rare occasions when they could all be together.

During the summer of 1874 Mother acquired an antiquated road wagon, the springs and upholstered seats of which were of fading grandeur. The Sisters thrilled at the sight of Mother riding it home behind an unambitious old cab horse whom she had rescued from oblivion. They named him Fritz. With this gear the nuns were better able to accept the provisions such as potatoes, bread, and flour offered in large quantities by generous farmers.

One day soon after, Mother arranged to take her wagonload of Sisters on a holiday touring the winding Mississippi and the farmlands to the west. With their Mother holding the reins rather perfunctorily, the Sisters relaxed completely, rejoicing in this wonderful example of God's bounty. As they approached the spreading acres tilled by Olaf Nielsen, they saw the farmer was standing at the edge of the dusty road. He motioned for them to halt and greeted them jovially. With varied reactions they observed he was trying to control a squealing pig under his left arm. "For you," he told them. "I give to you Sisters." His light blue eyes glistened merrily in the glare of sunlight enveloping them all.

"The Sisters are delighted with this donation," Mother tried to explain to the farmer, "but they have no way of getting him home safely, as he could easily jump out of our wagon." But the man would take no refusal. He was determined that the Sisters should have this fat little fellow, so he tied the pig in a sack and planted it securely in the wagon bed.

"Now he's safe," he said and wrinkled his dried up skin even more as he smiled.

The Sisters, trusting the farmer, set out for home. Old Fritz had a knack for finding all the ruts in the road. It seemed he never missed one of them. "You would think at his age and with his experience, he would stick to the smooth spots," said Sister Ludovica! They all laughed. Like a boat on a stormy ocean, the poor wagon bobbed up and down. A mile up the road, Sister Clara said she thought she heard something grunt. There it was again! Even Mother turned to see. Fearing to look, all the Sisters turned in the direction of the wagon bed. Out climbed the pig who ran to nuzzle his friendly pink snout affectionately into their skirts. Sister Clara let out a shriek which frightened old Fitz into a panic. Down the path he raced. In vain, Mother pulled in on the reins.

The incident might have ended in disaster had the Sisters not passed another farmhouse, where a farmer plowing in his fields took after the runaway horse. Finally the horse was quieted by the farmer and the pig again was secured. " 'Sister Pearl White,' that's what we should name you, Mother," Sister Josepha declared as the nervous group broke into rollicking laughter.

Winter 1874 had settled on the city of St. Louis. It fastened its tentacles on people as they rushed through the streets, the wind whipping around their legs. Snow mounds seemed to be growing like grass in spring. Everyone was resigned to the rigors of the coming months. Inside the castle-like convent on Gratiot Street Mother Odilia sat alone in a secluded alcove where she could meditate on the nuisance factors of maintaining a flourishing religious community amid a troubled world. Here, she could face and conquer the calamitous positions in which the Sisters of St. Mary repeatedly found themselves. At her tiny desk-table, pencil in hand, she worked over the congregation's situation. At last, laying down her work, she looked up to see the clean flakes dropping en masse again. She heard the December wind sweeping around the corners of the home, even through thick walls of brick. She thought painfully of the contrast between her own warmth and the sufferings of the poor she loved so dearly, hungry and discouraged as they inevitably were when she went to them. She was torn by the demands on her to shelter her community and provide it with the necessary firm foundation for further growth. Yet she wanted to be doing more and more for the poor and sick souls in St. Louis, who needed help so desperately. In love she wanted to run to them erratically and give everything of herself to help them. Yet sound logic told her it was best to make her object an organized charity, for only in this way, she realized reluctantly, could the most people in need be cared for in the best ways possible.

These cares weighed heavily on Mother. As she slipped her plump fingers under the rimless circles of glass to press down on her stinging eyes, she seemed an old woman. The short years since her migration had changed her appearance in great detail. Her body seemed shorter and heavier, accustomed to hard work. Her shoulders bowed as if to give a slight hint of a mighty burden placed on them. Mother's face had a serene look, yet vital and forceful. Her powerful eyes rose in rutted lines of compassion into her unmarked brow.

She thought of the constantly haranguing problem of money. The time had come for the December payment on the convent's mortgage. And she had as yet no part of the one thousand dollars that must be paid to the bank in another week. Still she had not yet had one regret about her intuitive decision to dash ahead and build the new house even before the money was available. Always, when the time came due, money came, too. But this time what should she do? With a sigh, she picked up her pen and began to unburden her heart to her faithful friend, St. Joseph. Her complete faith in him is revealed by her vexation at his unhurrying response to her daily beseeching.

My Holy Father!
I am in sore distress! In the name of thy dear Son Who has never refused me nor anyone when asked in His name, I beg of thee to grant my request.

Within eight days, we must have one thousand dollars. You must help us; you can if you will. The Sacred Heart is propitious to us. We have consecrated ourselves anew to Him today. Tell Him of our need at once; He will not refuse you anything.

87

In thanksgiving, I will give your poor souls seven holy Masses and seven times the Way of the Cross. But you must help at once; the people need their money. You must give us the money; we do not want to BORROW any more as we have debts enough already.

Asking this favor once more in the Name of Jesus, I remain,
                                    Your most unworthy child,
                                    Mother Odilia.

As she confidently folded the missive and slipped it into an envelope her eyes fell on a piece of fine paper lying before her which reminded her that the year 1874, now drawing to an end, had been a most important one in the annals of the Community. She picked up the formal document which announced publicly, bringing particular joy to the Gratiot Street house, that in the previous November the Sisters' new title had been recognized and that the Community had been incorporated under the Laws of Missouri as Sisters of St. Mary of the Third Order of St. Francis.

All temptations to be discouraged faded as she counted out the many blessings and accomplishments of her band. For another year her Sisters had labored tirelessly to allay the ravages of the epidemics, and none had been stricken with either smallpox or cholera. The 20 Sisters nursed 266 patients. Always the sick poor were being cared for. The Novitiate and Convent were flourishing and, with ecclesiastical guidance, their spiritual life was progressing. The home for unwed mothers provided the refuge intended, despite the great hardship it brought for the Sisters operating it.

She rose to deliver her letter to St. Joseph in the chapel. Meeting her in the hall was Sister Agnes. Mother could see there were tears in her eyes. "What is wrong, my dear?" Mother asked, concerned.

"It's a wonderful thing, Mother, really. I don't mean to cry. It just overwhelms me to be a part of such demonstrations of the power of God. You see, a man came to the door just now and asked for me. When I answered Sister Rose's call, I found Mr. Mueller waiting. You remember him, Mother, the one who when I asked him for money for our work once practically threw me out of his house; but when his family came down with smallpox, I was sent to care for them. Well, just now he came and simply thanked us and gave me all this money. A thousand dollars. Is it a miracle, Mother?"

"Now, my child, do not say such things," admonished the relieved Superior, as she took the money and continued on her way to the chapel.

It was Christmas again! Mother herself arranged the nativity figures around the crib. Early that morning all the Community had gathered to sing "Ihr Kinderlein Kommet." "The birthday of the Little King is always a joyous as well as a holy day the world over, even in the poorest of convents," Mother reminded the Sisters. "Let us in our impoverished convent try to model our religious lives on the life of the Christ Child Himself."

That evening when Mother Odilia did not appear in the refectory for the gala Christmas supper, questioning glances found their way to her worn empty chair at the head of the table. After grace had been said, Sister Magdalene answered their wordless question.

"Mother is ill tonight. We do not know how serious it is, but Dr. Miller is coming over. Her skin is very hot, she must have a high temperature and she seems to have a rash which is spreading."

The gay house took on the atmosphere of a hermitage as everyone walked on tiptoe and spoke in subdued tones. Their worst fears were realized that evening when Doctor Miller reported that Mother had typhoid fever.

Sister Magdalene herself took over the nursing care. Many were the precautions she used to prevent the spread of this insidious disease. Through five long weeks she stayed at Mother's side, bringing her gradually through the various stages of the siege, while the Sisters at home and at their duties fervently prayed that their Mother be spared.

During the worst stages of Mother's illness word was received at the convent from Sister Elizabeth who led the work among the smallpox victims in St. Charles, that Father Koch himself had been stricken and died in late January, 1875. "Strangely enough," she continued, "the epidemic has subsided. We find our work here nearly finished and plan now to return home as soon as possible."

By March, Sister Magdalene announced that Mother would soon be able to return to work. On the Sunday afternoon when she first was permitted to sit with her daughters downstairs in the community room her heart was jubilant. "There is so much work to be done," she told herself sternly, "I must gain my strength back soon." As she was helped to her chair at the head of the table all the Sisters sang to her. When she spied Sister Elizabeth and her "missionaries" crowded in among the novices far down the table, she could hardly trust her vision. "This is truly a homecoming," she told the beaming group.

Amid all the exchanges of news and embraces, Mother had a sudden realization of how crowded the convent had become. She counted 27 Sisters and seven candidates. There were scarcely enough chairs for them all. If even one more girl asked for admission there wouldn't be a bed for her. "Of course, that would not matter too much," Mother reflected, "because she could always have my bed. How the little Community has grown in the past three years; we have actually doubled our number! And now the third floor dormitories that had seemed so spacious are full." Sister Vincent's cry of delight brought Mother from her reverie.

"Look, Mother, I'm almost as tall as Sister Theresa now. I've grown almost two inches in the last six months."

Later that night, Mother thought seriously on the matter. Something had to be done. Like the old woman in the shoe she had many children. But unlike the old lady in the shoe, she DID know what to do. She would go to St. Joseph. He must help them!

Taking up her long black pen, she dipped it vigorously into the watery ink. Slowly and carefully she wrote her plan:

Dearest Father, St. Joseph,
Thou seest how large our family has grown. We need a larger house. If thou wilt give us a larger place, then sell "Lowell"

so that the community will not suffer loss for thou knowest we
are poor and it was bought with hard earned money.

Your loving child,
Mother Odilia.

This message was placed in the hand of St. Joseph. He had
no excuse for not seeing it, she reminded him before she left; there
it was in his hand.

May 1875 arrived in sweet remembrance of Mary's glory and
of another clothing day for the aspiring young Postulants. Mother
listed six generous souls ready for the investiture ceremonies. Their
six months in the order had been spent at the bedside of God's
forsaken as well as in prayer and instruction, which now was becoming more possible with the growth of the Community. "Six,"
Mother marvelled. "We were only six two and a half years ago.
Ah, the fervor of young hearts is so inspiring to me in my time of
trial. Having tasted the cup of bitterness, they beg for a bigger
quaff. As our work load increases, so do our vocations. Only they
who have put their lips to the cup know of its sweetness, and the
inebriation of it is reserved for those who generously tilt and drain
the cup."

May 29, 1875 marked the formal entrance into the Sisters
of St. Mary of Sisters Seraphia Schlochtermeyer, Mechtildis Danner,
Petronilla McCloud, Stanislaus Dickmann, Vincent Hickey, and
Gonzaga Flescherin.

That same spring several articles attacking the dogma of the
Immaculate Conception appeared in a German secular newspaper
published in St. Louis, the *Amerika*. Thoroughly aroused, Mother
Odilia made a personal visit to the editor himself, a Mr. August
Preuss, defending the dogma and asking that the articles be recalled. Preuss, astonished at Mother's faith and courage, subse-
quently acquiesced. Through a friendship which later developed
between them Preuss gained an interest in the Catholic faith that
led to his conversion, that of his three sons, and his business part-
ner, John Roselein. Preuss' three sons eventually became Jesuit
priests.

About this time a young girl with a fervent desire to join Mother Odilia's work among the sick poor came to the Convent of the Sisters of St. Mary under unusual circumstances. The incident is described in the early records of the Community in this way:

Laughter filled the warm spring air as the students filed in disorderly lines out the front door of the Marien Schule in the gay town of Leipzig, Germany. For thirty of them it was graduation day; that meant a turning point in their lives. The graduating class, forming several small groups, were engaged in animated conversation. They were discussing their various plans. A number of girls had made arrangements to enter convents in the nearby town. Gertrude wanted to be a nun too, a nursing sister, but she could not decide which congregation to enter.

Soon after, paging idly through the local paper, she came across a "card of thanks" to the Sisters of St. Mary in America from a grateful family whom they had nursed through a siege of smallpox. This was the Community for her. She was so convinced of it, that all the while she lay in bed waiting for sleep to come, she made her plans. When she did fall asleep, she dreamed of her adventure.

In her dream, she had arrived in St. Louis and was looking for the Convent. She found the house, but it was empty as the Sisters were all out on missions of love. She saw a Sister come, take a key from its nail by the window frame and go into the house.

Next day, Gertrude told her parents of her desire to enter this convent in St. Louis. There was much opposition, of course, both from her parents and her pastor, who felt that she should enter a community in her own country. But Gertrude had heard His call and was determined to follow it. After a year of fervent prayer and entreaties, her parents finally agreed.

When she arrived at the convent in St. Louis, she was stunned to discover the key hanging on a nail by the window frame just as it had appeared in her dream. But what was more astounding was that the Sister she had seen in her dream was none other than Mother Odilia herself.

CHAPTER EIGHT

Her Children Rose Up and Called Her Blessed

In the early part of 1876, a regal black carriage came to a gentle stop before the home of one of Mother Odilia's first friends in America, the Reverend Henry Muehlsiepen. A crisp-looking driver alighted from the seat and supported a feeble but expensively dressed old lady as she descended. He handed her a pearl-handled cane on which she depended heavily as she ascended the stone steps leading to the rectory. The servant man returned to guard the behavior of the pair of horses as he perched on the front of the barouche.

Father Muehlsiepen greeted the noted Mrs. Elizabeth Schiller with affection. The wealthy woman had a reputation for her charity to the poor. Sensing that she had come on some such mission this very day, he asked her to sit with him in the parlor over a cup of tea.

"Father," she began, seating herself with a sigh, "there has been a desire in my old heart for a long time now and I will have no peace until I see it realized. Ever since Henry died, which will be ten years next month, I have been living alone in that big house. It seems such a waste; all those empty rooms and all that land."

"Yes," Father agreed, watching her closely as she sat erect, her hands together on the cane held in front of her.

"I love children so much," she continued, in a shaky voice. "Of the six God blessed me with, none are now living." A tear fell from the bleary, gray eyes and trickled down the wrinkled cheek. Daintily she brushed it aside with her gloved hand. She was not the type of woman to feel sorry for herself; bravely she went on in a cheerful tone.

"I've come to a decision this morning, Father, and I know you will help me."

"If I am able, yes, Mrs. Schiller," he said patiently.

"I am getting too old to be of much use, and Henry's fortune is just about gone, so I want to turn my home over to someone who will convert it into a refuge for the poor orphans—there are so many now, you know." Then, as if reading his thoughts, she went on, "All I ask in return is my meals and the use of two rooms in the north wing as living quarters."

Father Muehlsiepen did not speak for such a long time that the widow felt he disliked her coming to him with this proposal. Father's thoughts had gone instinctively to the leader of the Sisters of St. Mary who had helped him time and time again when he had work to be done. She would be thrilled with the prospect of a home for orphans and as a donation at that, he was positive, knowing as he did how working among children again would appeal to her mother's heart. Still so many objections came to mind. "How could I ask Mother to take over yet another job? The very idea is preposterous. To see her so prematurely old is painful enough already. I should be planning to relieve her of some of her work, not trying to ask more help of her. And then, even if she should agreed to this undertaking, where would the money come from for the upkeep of the house. I know that Mother's Community has long since exhausted their funds and their members in charitable work demanded by the sick and poor of St. Louis daily."

Another spirit seemed to move the cleric to want to at least talk the proposal over with Mother Odilia to see what her thoughts on it would be. As for the money problem, he already knew what Mother would say to that. "Don't worry about where the money will come from. The money will come when we need it — from God."

St. Joseph's Home — 1876

Mother Odilia (right) is shown among some of the orphans cared for at St. Joseph's Home. The woman in the center is believed to be Mrs. Schiller.

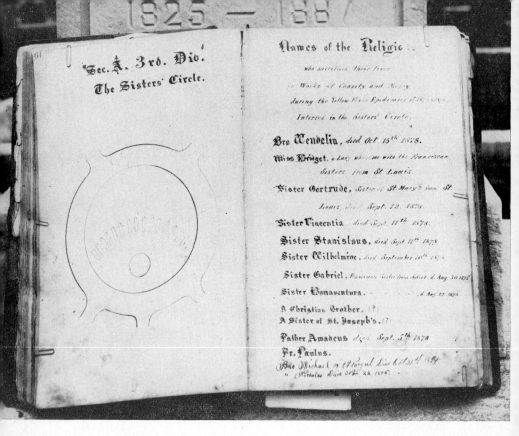

The book containing the ground plans of the cemetery in Memphis and showing the names of Sisters of St. Mary among those of others who gave their lives in helping those stricken with the dread yellow fever in 1878.

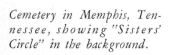

Cemetery in Memphis, Tennessee, showing "Sisters' Circle" in the background.

Father turned abruptly from pacing the room as he deliberated. He had almost forgotten that Mrs. Schiller was still sitting on the horsehair couch waiting for his answer.

"Yes, yes, Mrs. Schiller," he replied resolutely, "I know just where I can find a community who will be happy to take over your house and use it as an orphan home. I will drop around to see you in the morning with a decision. Today I must contact these good people and acquaint them with this new project."

When Reverend Muehlsiepen arrived late that afternoon, he found Mother Odilia, her sleeves rolled up, with her apron on. They talked as she prepared a scanty meal for the few who would be coming later.

"Well, good evening, Reverend Father," Mother greeted, trying to hide her surprise, for she knew that only something very unusual would bring him to their convent at that hour.

"Good evening, Mother, may I see you for a few minutes?" he asked hesitantly for now that he had arrived and witnessed, although he already knew, the exhaustion on her face, he feared to make his request.

"Mother," he began quickly, "do you think you could take on another work of charity — I mean . . ."

Mother was facing him now; her thin, loose veil moving slightly in the pleasant breeze coming in the open windows. She had aged these past years, indeed; yet, her kind brown eyes had not. They would never change; it seemed as though her soul was speaking through them and her soul spoke only one language, the language of love and service to others through love.

Father explained his meeting with the generous dowager to Mother. She sat with hands clasped tightly around her crucifix for a moment after he had finished. Father had been very frank with her, explaining that there would be no financial support for the home except what they obtained by begging.

Unfolding her roughened hands, Mother replied in the low tone she was accustomed to use. It was not much more than a whisper now, but it was impregnated with a determination that inspired confidence.

"Yes, Father, we will be glad to accept this added burden. Of course, at present, I really don't know how we shall manage, but God will provide a way."

As soon as the priest left, Mother went straight to St. Joseph and prayed to him. "A thousand times I thank you, dear St. Joseph. Now we will have a larger house and we can sell Lowell, but," she added, shaking her finger, "you realize, I am sure, how we are putting ourselves in even more debt and we certainly expect you to get us out of it," she warned him. As an afterthought, she added, "I shall try to name the new orphanage in your honor."

Back in the kitchen, the potatoes were cooked to mush; but Mother could not tell what she was eating that night anyway, as her mind was far from the food before her.

The contract was properly drawn up and the palacious property deeded to the Sisters of St. Mary by Mrs. Schiller. It consisted of ten acres near the junction of Arsenal Street and Arkansas Avenue with a large residence and two smaller buildings, one frame and the other stone. In the brick house there were eight large and two small rooms, an attic, and a good cellar. Two of these rooms, with a folding door between them, were arranged for a chapel.

The frame building was furnished for the older children while the babies were comfortably housed in the stone dwelling which was called "Nazareth."

The Sisters took possession of their new home on July 4, 1876. Henceforth it was known as St. Joseph's Home and Mother-house of the Sisters of St. Mary, with the convent on Gratiot remaining as another house for the order. It was an ideal home, they all agreed. There was a fine orchard, a vineyard, and a large tract of land which would be a garden. Thus they were relieved of some of the care for a livelihood although this new labor of working in the fields to eke out a mere sustenance for themselves and their charges required strenuous effort on the part of the Sisters.

But the arduous duties of the Sisters were compensated for by their spiritual activities which they now could carry on more as they desired.

Mother Odilia was happy with her new home and the chance to establish still another home for little ones as well. We read in the chronicals

> In Saint Louis, after the solemn services in the Catholic Churches, a grand parade was held over the principal streets of the city, celebrating the golden episcopal jubilee of Pope Pius IX. Father Faerber, with three other priests, occupied a carriage drawn by four white horses. Four open carriages followed with the children of St. Joseph's Home. The girls wore blue dresses, white and yellow sashes and turbans of the same color.

In October of that year, following the sale of "La Crêsche" in Lowell to the Sisters of the Good Shepherd, plans were drawn up by Groesse and Remmers, architects and builders, who were staunch supporters of Mother's work in St. Louis, for an additional three-story building to be completed within a few months. The first story would be used for laundry purposes, equipment for which in those days did not require much space. The second floor was arranged for additional Sisters' dormitories, and the third, for more children's sleeping rooms.

Upon its completion, Mother was justly proud of the new addition. She wrote to a friend at this time:

> My Dear,
>
> I have watched last night again with a dying woman and must force my sleepy head for thoughts to write this letter; but I must tell you that the addition to St. Joseph's Home is finished and it is beautiful!
>
> We will have a hard battle paying it off, but I place all my trust in the good God.
>
> In the past year, we have taken care of 325 families with smallpox, cholera, and all kinds of diseases. In this way, we build up our little convent day and night in strict service to God. His blessing is with us.
>
> Dear St. Joseph is a great help to me. He refused nothing that I asked of him. You should see what a beautiful statue we have of him on the second floor of our convent, all deco-

rated with flowers. We call this part of our home, "Joseph's Hill."

At the entrance stands Blessed Mother, as big as St. Joseph. . . ."

The chapel at St. Joseph's Home was a veritable flower garden on the morning of November 21, 1876, the feast of the Presentation of our Lady. A benefactor, Henry Shaw, the later famous owner of Shaw's botanical gardens in St. Louis, had donated a gorgeous array of flowers for the solemn reception day rites, as he had done for the Sisters on so many other occasions. Mother had spent much time yesterday draping and arranging the assortment of sprays, buds, and blossoms. She loved to work with flowers, feeling that she was scattering God's magnificence throughout His house.

Mother witnessed the investiture of six postulants who took the religious names of Sisters Mary Johanna Magenheimer, Henrica Nicholay, Aloysia Schruefer, Genevieve Berback, Xaveria Muren, and Cunigunda Schulz. The vivacious girls revelled in their new black wool habit, with its veil and poplin cape. Beneath this cape was a short brown scapular, on top of it hung their crucified Spouse to show all the world their choice of Lovers. The Sisters now all wore rosaries with large black beads. The rosary hung to the left, the symbolic red cincture with its knots and tassles, to the right. The knots, they learned, were a perpetual reminder that they had bound themselves to their dear Spouse in a very close union; the tassels were representative of the instruments of His Sacred Passion. Reverend Muehlsiepen officiated at the ceremony, assisted by Fathers William Faerber and Philip Lotz.

The community had incurred much expense in the additions and remodeling necessary at St. Joseph's. Since the collecting tours in St. Louis were no longer substantial enough, permission was obtained by Mother Odilia to solicit alms through the Midwest in the Dioceses of Wisconsin, Iowa, and Minnesota. Sisters Mary Seraphia, Gertrude, Magdalene, and Petronilla were chosen to make this sacrifice of leaving home which they did with generous hearts. Mother, relying on her own experience as a mendicant, was uniquely able to equip her spiritual daughters for this difficult task.

Sister Johanna and Sister Ludovica who were collecting at home in St. Louis would tramp the streets all day; often they would wait outside factories and stores begging in His name. When dark fell, they were glad to return to the convent. Tired, hungry, and frequently discouraged, the Sisters would bring their charity to Mother. Some days they were fortunate to collect a dollar. "How can a Community exist on that, much less support an orphanage?" they asked Mother Odilia.

Many strange incidents happened to the Sisters on these collecting trips and sometimes they came home with the most unexpected "donations." This was the case with Sister Henrica one day while she was begging in Union Station on Twelfth and Poplar Streets.

In the center of the station stood a huge, red-faced policeman who was apparently in distress. He was walking forward and backward, just a few yards in each direction, but always on his forward trek he would stare at the nun. Sister Henrica saw him and felt uneasy. "After all," she told herself, "he could not arrest me for we have been properly authorized to do this soliciting." Finally the burly officer advanced boldly toward her tipping his hat. "Well," thought Sister, "that's a relief. I don't see handcuffs, unless he has . . ."

"Sister," spoke up Officer Mulley as he identified himself, "would you help me with a problem?"

"Why, yes, if I can, sir."

"And sure you can," he assured her. "You see, it's like this. A few hours ago, a woman in here asked a colored lady named Mrs. Boggs who lives in a shack down by the tracks, to hold her baby while she bought a ticket. But the woman never came back for the baby. The Boggs woman took the little one home and then called me. Now, what am I to do? Sure, I represent the law but . . ." Taking off his helmet he scratched his head as he formed

99

his request, "I was wondering if you would come with me to get the baby and take it to your orphanage."

"Yes, of course, officer," Sister replied confidently, pocketing a dime that a passerby handed to her. "Fifty cents today! Oh yes, fifty cents and a baby. Another boarder!" she mused as she hastened to Arsenal Street away from the dank, dark house. The infant boy, just a week old, was very sick from exposure and improper feeding. Because he was not expected to live, Mother Odilia took the responsibility of baptizing the child at once, giving him the name Henry Joseph Mayrose.

One year after his admission to the Home, the little boy was still so weak and emaciated that it was necessary to carry him about on a pillow. Sister Stanislaus, his special nurse, was sadly discouraged with his progress. So, on his first birthday, she carried Henry Joseph into the chapel and placed him on the altar steps and prayed, "Dear Lord, relieve this child of his miseries, I beg You. But if he is destined to do some good in this world, then please let him get well soon. I ask it through Your love of children to whom You always gave a special blessing. I ask it through the tender heart of Your Mother who must be moved by compassion by the plight of this little one. I ask it through St. Joseph whose name he proudly bears."

Then carrying the baby back to its tiny basket, she kissed him goodnight. In the days that followed, Henry Joseph's health improved rapidly, miraculously. He became a strong chubby fellow and when he was five years old was adopted by a good Catholic family. "Perhaps God has some special work for him to do," it was felt by the Sisters as they watched the new family happily depart.

CHAPTER NINE

She Hath Stretched Out
Her Hands to the Poor

T HE CITY OF St. Louis in the year 1877 behaved like a
weathercock, testifying to the future grandeur of the entire Midwest. The influx of immigrants continued from all parts of Europe, but especially from Germany. Farm people, as well, came
by the thousands to become a part of the new urban industry. These
new people had, since the closing of the Civil War, swelled the
population of St. Louis from a third to two-thirds of a million.
Building was at its peak; business was booming; everywhere industry was bringing change to the adolescent city.

Problems naturally accompanied the rapid growth. Yet, the
factors produced by the present state of things as Mother Mary
Odilia took stock of her five years of work in America, brought a
state of crisis to the Sisters of St. Mary.

First of all, the unending procession of new faces into the
city, the sight of every one of which reminded Mother's compas-
sionate heart of her own hard immigration, meant that the crowded
tenements and makeshift shacks were being relied upon ever more.
The sickness and disease which repeatedly struck the city helpless
were thereby strengthened in their ruthless powers. The Sisters
were experiencing difficulties from many sources in nursing the
sick in their homes, especially among the poorer classes. Often
the bare necessities of life were wanting in the poorest homes, and

the patient's own surroundings were a hindrance to his recovery. Properly prepared food might help the patient make rapid strides along the highway of health, but in these hovels of the poor one would do well to find bread and a little fresh meat.

The most frightening factor of all was that with the boom nearly everyone in the large city who ordinarily could be depended on by Mother for substantial help was now preoccupied in gambling his financial status on the projected status of the city. This meant that now, when the Sisters needed funds more than ever before, the money was not coming in. "Why," Mother Odilia told herself in alarm, "we even have difficulty getting a doctor to donate his services. And worse, without money we cannot buy medicine for our patients. We are stopped everywhere by an insurmountable brick wall," she moaned to her dear St. Joseph as she knelt in the chapel early one morning.

The brick wall was threatening the very existence of the Community as well, for even the Community burse to provide food for the Sisters' daily frugal meals was nearly exhausted. Mother Odilia's eyes were glazed by a deep preoccupation for a long time. Finally, the dream that had always dwelt like a shadow in her mind's recesses began to take a definite form. "We must crumble the wall," Mother spoke aloud. "We must build one of our own, a wall that will stop disaster and disease at our doorstep. St. Louis needs a hospital to care in the most efficient way for all victims of our epidemics. We must build a hospital—make it a home both for ourselves and our sick poor. Instead of going to the homes of our patients, we shall have a place now where they can come to us."

Her determined spirit fired up by this new purpose, Mother contacted her constant friend and adviser, Father Faerber who, in turn, met with several civic and ecclesiastical leaders to discuss the plan. The hospital movement was quite popular in the United States by this time. Mother's would not, of course, be the first hospital to be established in St. Louis. But it would be the first hospital given primarily over to caring for epidemic victims, especially smallpox, typhoid, and cholera.

Backed up by the consent of her superiors and the enthusiastic support of interested lay people, Mother Odilia boldly purchased a suitable property on Papin Street and, still wondering where the money would come from, gave orders to builders on how she wished the building to be renovated.

On May 24 of the same year, the feast of Our Lady, help of Christians, came a memorable day in the chronicles of the Congregation of the Sisters of St. Mary. The air was heavy with the sweet fragrance of spring blossoms and numerous bouquets which filled the newly painted chapel in the hospital. White snapdragons on the altar were opening their mouths in tribute to the King. The Sisters in single file moved into the small chapel. Reverend Henry Muehlsiepen had already blessed the building and the chapel dedicated to our Mother of Sorrows. Father Faerber prepared to celebrate the first holy Mass here. Dr. T. L. Papin, Sr., one of the first to offer to help staff the new hospital without any fee, served at the altar. St. Mary's Infirmary, as the new hospital was called, opened its doors to six new patients.

Mother showed the priest and guests around the new facilities pointing out the care which had been taken to maintain sanitary conditions in the wards and operating and supply rooms as well. She had made it a habit to study the newest methods of hospital care in preparation for this great day. Sister Clara, she explained, although she had been in the order but a year, was a trained nurse, and would move efficiently into the position of authority in the hospital.

Among the members of the first medical staff of St. Mary's Infirmary who offered their services gratis were: Doctors Louis Bauer, B. M. Hypes, T. W. Holland, Charles Garcia, Sr., Mordiacai Yarnall, A. C. Robinson, Rudolph Gebser, William Frazier, F. L. Stuerver and Papin. Most of them had been the Sisters' mainstays already in their home nursing as well.

From experience, Mother knew what would be necessary for the successful management of this brick rectangle three stories high called a hospital. She had shown great foresight in her prepa-

rations. The Sisters became officially trained nurses under the tute-
lage of the staff doctors. "A hospital must have a pharmacy and
a druggist," Mother Odilia insisted. Dr. Charles Garcia offered
to teach one of the Sisters the pharmaceutical science; Sister Aloysia
Schruefer, who was later to become Mother General of the order,
was chosen as the first pupil. Sister made rapid progress under
him, for in those days preparations were quite simple. In order to
economize, Sister learned, roots and herbs had to be macerated and
powdered to make extracts, tinctures, and other remedies. She
learned, too, to roll pills, for sugar-coated pills were not developed
then.

That evening, sitting at the window of her bare room in St.
Joseph's home, Mother smiled in deep satisfaction — satisfaction
of a dream come true, a hope realized. She was thinking that now
she and her Sisters could give even more of themselves to Christ's
suffering ones. She felt in a way like the little girl in Regen long
ago, box of ointment in hand, eager to heal the wounds of the
world.

She knew fully that suffering is a cross. She would continue
to make every effort to lighten its load for the sick. She knew, too,
about the added hardship of being poor, unable to buy medicine
or care. The sick poor she would likewise continue, she decided,
to make special objects of all the charity her Congregation could
offer.

Mother had repeated many times to her spiritual daughters,
"The cross is a mighty voice." She knew that the sick above all
could hear it if they would. And if they could be taught to love
it, could be convinced of the truth of the words of the Curé of Ars,
"The cross is God's gift to His friends," then she and her Sisters
would be amply rewarded for all their hardships. She was thinking, too, of the tremendous debt they had contracted and of the
limited numbers of Sisters which now had to be divided between
their three works of charity.

It had grown dark all around. Slowly Mother got up to light
the lamp and draw the shade. "Yes," she said to herself, "the cross

is a mighty voice and it never speaks more loudly than during sickness or misfortune. How much more good we can now do for the souls of men because we will have, not a sporadic contact with them, as when nursing in homes, but one that is constant; all day and every day. And this, when the voice of the cross is loudest."

Mother Odilia sighed. Oh, if only she could afford to staff more than just one hospital, but some day maybe. . . . Picking up her rosary beads from the window ledge, she knelt by the hard bed and kissing the crucifix, she was glad. Glad that she and her Sisters were partners with Him in His tremendous mission of healing. Healing both of body and soul.

During the first seven months of its operation, St. Mary's Infirmary cared for sixty patients. Thirty-six of these were entered on the record as "Our dear Lord's patient." This meant, of course, that they were the very poor and could pay nothing.

Most of the sick which they cared for up to now in private homes were afflicted with either smallpox, cholera, scarlet fever, yellow fever, typhoid fever, or diphtheria. Those unfortunate individuals who were shunned by the great majority of their fellow men, sometimes even by their own families. And now that the Sisters had opened their own hospital, many of the patients who filled its beds suffered from the same diseases and tuberculosis as well. Perhaps this is the reason that Mother Odilia took as one of her special advocates the humble St. Roch, patron of contagious diseases. Even up to our own day the Sisters petition him daily for preservation from "contagion of soul and body."

St. Roch, whose statue stands in the Motherhouse chapel today, was born in the year 1295 of a noble family in Montpellier, France. At the age of 20, he undertook a pilgrimage to Rome and while in Italy witnessed the horrors of a smallpox plague. Like another St. Francis of Assisi, he renounced his wealth and courageously offered his youth to the service of the victims of the black death. At Piasenza, he too, became afflicted with the sickness and dragged himself into a nearby forest where he prepared himself for death. But God was not to be outdone in generosity. He sent a dog with food and drink to him daily, thus providing nourishment until his recovery. When the saint did recover, he returned to his native Montpellier to convalesce. But there he was unaccountably arrested as a spy and cast into prison where he died in the year 1327. To Mother he seemed a renegade in the eyes of men but a saint in the eyes of God!

Mother Odilia saw that St. Mary's Infirmary was running at a fairly smooth pace. She herself continued to reside at St. Joseph's Home which was the motherhouse of the Community as well as the orphans' home. Every Friday she made a practice of traveling to St. Mary's Convent and to the Infirmary to give spiritual conferences to the Sisters. One particular week in which fell the great feast of Corpus Christi, she arrived two days early at the Infirmary to help the Sisters prepare for the Thursday rituals. The commemoration of the Institution of the Holy Eucharist was another of Mother Odilia's many favorite holy days.

"Good boy, good boy," Mother complimented old Fritz affectionately as she climbed down from the spring wagon. The old horse turned his head as if to acknowledge the kindness.

Every year for this feast Mother and her Sisters would take evergreen branches gathered from the countryside and twine the full, shaggy limbs into huge wreaths which they hung on the pillars and walls of the chapel.

Today the new chapel was being treated to a glimpse of the love that filled Mother's heart for her Spouse. Late into the night she worked, twining and tying branches, climbing ladders, ignoring scratched hands. It was worth the effort, she concluded, standing off to view the effect this particular night. No, it wasn't perfect, but it certainly was close to it the laughing group agreed.

After the work followed a prayer period in which Mother Odilia began her homily by reminding her Sisters of an important fact which she always stressed in her talks to young novices. "There are but two virtues insisted on in the New Testament," she said, "honesty and selfless devotion in love. You Sisters as well as I are doing the work of God here today because we loved our Creator enough some time ago to give up our lives to Him so that His work might be carried on. You know that God, in the very beginning of time, created the world in order that Christ might be glorified. Without anticipating the birth — and death — of

Christ, our own beloved spouse, God would not have been moved to do the work of creation. Christ was meant to be our Redeemer. He bore the responsibility of bringing sanctification to us. So, as he did so, he earned the right of authority over us. Our obedience must be to Him, and it follows to all his delegates, for this reason. Now, in order that Christ will be glorified," Mother took a deep sigh as she formed her thoughts, "we are given the opportunity to share in His priesthood. This we prepare ourselves for by constantly striving after the special virtue of selfless loving of our fellowmen which we have every opportunity here in our work to do. Christ Himself gives us the first share of His holy priesthood in baptism. Today I wish to remind you that the Mass is the focal point of our work, of our prayers and of our existence. But especially is the Holy Eucharist, whose institution we venerate tomorrow, the very climax of all these things."

Overnight, leisurely and calm Memphis had become a frightened city, stalked as it was by the ruthless monster, yellow fever. In August, 1878, the newspaper was full of reports of the march through Louisiana and Mississippi of the dread disease which had snuffed out so many lives in the previous sieges of 1867 and 1873.

Memphis Health Commissioner Doctor John Erskine established quarantine stations immediately. These quarantine observances meant that no one was allowed to leave the city proper; no steamboat was allowed to stop for two hundred miles above and below Memphis on the Mississippi river. Inland trains were permitted to stop at no depot nearer than Louisville, Kentucky, 391 miles away. Immediately, a group of prominent citizens who had organized forces in the city to combat the sickness, sent out a nation-wide appeal for doctors, nurses, food, medicine, and clothing. The men called themselves the Howard Association of Memphis, Tennessee. They had been formed when the first plague had settled on Memphis in 1867.

By August 14, the Howard Association took complete charge of the affairs of the stricken city. They pledged themselves to the care of the sick, relief of the suffering, and burial of the dead.

As Mother Odilia opened her Memphis postmarked letter and read this appeal she saw the feverish, writhing body of the crucified Christ in each poor victim. She wanted to help the people of Memphis, but how dare she even suggest it. Did her Sisters not already have more work on their hands now than they could cope with? As she knelt in prayer her soul was filled with trust and courage. That evening she asked, "Would any of the Sisters be willing to go to Memphis to nurse the yellow fever victims."

There were many volunteers, for the generous hearts in this young Community responded to her example and could not refuse a request. Mother chose only five from the group: Sisters Margaret Mary Noelker, Wilhelmine Brinker, Gertrude Hentsches, Stanislaus Dickmann and Vincent Hickey — all were American-born Sisters, newly-professed and very young.

On August 30, after receiving the blessing of Reverend Patrick J. Ryan, co-adjutor Bishop of St. Louis, they left the city accompanied by Doctor Paul Nugent, a young physician interested in the disease.

They were little prepared for the spectacle that met their eyes. In the words of Father Quinn, a good priest of Memphis, who was seeing the scourge for the third time:

> To a stranger, the aspect of Memphis was most disheartening. The principal thoroughfares, as well as the lanes and alleys, were saturated with lime, carbolic acid, and other ill-odored disinfectants. The streets were obscured with the smoke of ignited tar and other evaporant combustibles with a view to dissipate the spores. Bedsteads, ticks, and blankets might be seen burning at almost every street corner.
>
> You might walk or ride several miles on Main Street, the principal thoroughfare, and see five people. Appearances lent an air of dreariness to the scene.
>
> To get a good idea of Memphis, one should enter one of the street cars. It would seem that every composite that emitted a disgusting smell was in requisition. While some outvied their proximate neighbors in the lavish use of cologne, musk and rosewater; others, armed with onions or asafoetida, seemed to issue a challenge to the nasal organs of the passengers. Even if an epidemic did not exist at all, one would react ominously

to see men and women on the cars, having large sponges attached to their noses; while others, primed with narcotics or alcoholic stimulants, acted like maniacs.

If the human mind was not capable of bearing much, it would certainly give way, seeing the huge piles or, rather, mountains of coffins in front of each undertaker's shop. The only evidence of living humanity seemed to be the hearses and the vehicles carrying the dead to the different cemeteries. Here, it was nothing unusual to see fifty coffins awaiting burial.

Howling of dogs, the piteous mewing of cats and the lowing of cattle, left behind by their owners, would almost convey an idea of the last judgment.

Pitiful and heart-rending scenes were every day encountered. The cries and wails of the bereaved mothers, wives, children, and husbands melted the stoutest heart. The ravings of some savored of blasphemy as they challenged the Almighty to give them a greater stroke. While some patients died smiling, laughing, or weeping, others, with the insatiable thirst, felt as though their blood and entrails were boiling. Hope of recovery was abandoned only when the black vomit appeared a few minutes before death. In many cases entire families were wiped out. . .

This was the frightful condition of the town on that morning of September 1, 1878, when the five Sisters arrived.

Although Memphis was predominantly Protestant, having at the time 53 Protestant and 5 Catholic Churches, its people welcomed the good Sisters as if they were angels. Upon their arrival, the five religious were taken to the Dominican convent.

On the way to the convent Sister Vincent, who was returning to her home town, caught sight of her own father. Her heart leaped in joy! She would have liked to stop to talk to him but the street car jogged along, permitting to them both only a fleeting glance and a wave of the hand. That she had come to Memphis to labor in the pain-wracked city, the father, John Hickey, knew; what he did not know was that she had offered this sacrifice for his conversion for he had fallen away from the faith many years before.

A Franciscan priest, Father Aloysius Wiewer, learned of the Sisters' whereabouts and came to the convent to prevail on some of them to go with him to the monastery.

Here distress had reached its climax. Reverend Aloysius was the only well person in the house. Father Maternus Mallman and Brothers Wendeline Kuemmerle and Amandus Yung were very sick; Brother Erasmus Hesse was dying. Father Maternus and Brothers Erasmus and Amandus died within a few days of each other, despite the nuns' ministrations.

When it became known in the city that the Sisters of St. Mary from St. Louis had come to lend their assistance, calls for them to nurse some stricken family came pouring in from all over Memphis. The regret and sorrow of the Sisters in being obliged to refuse so many families may well be imagined.

An urgent request came from the Howard Association for a nurse to care for the Simms family. Mr. Simms was a highly respected citizen of Memphis and a founding member of the Association. Sister Vincent answered the need that same night.

As the good Sisters of St. Mary labored day and night in the poorly ventilated houses with little time for rest, the dread monster was hovering near them unnoticed. Not until he had even them clenched tightly in his vice-like grip did they realize that they too were ill.

On September 8, just one week after their arrival, Sister Margaret Mary, with tears in her eyes, penned this letter to Mother Odilia:

Dear Reverend Mother,

It makes me feel bad that I must send you such sad news. Four of our dear Sisters are very sick, Sisters Stanislaus, Wilhelmine, Gertrude, and Vincent. Sister Vincent was nursing Mrs. Simms and we are not able to bring her home; her temperature is 105 degrees.

The other three Sisters are in a room here. From the little window one can see the high altar in the Church. We have at present seven patients in the house. I am writing this sitting with Father Maternus who is very low.

110

A never-failing friend, our Mother of Perpetual Help.

SANDERS-CO.S

St. Alphonsus "Rock" Church, St. Louis, in 1880. It was to this church, three miles from St. Joseph's Home, that Mother Odilia and her Sisters walked to invoke the aid of our Lady of Perpetual Help in obtaining the recognition and approbation of the Holy See.

The original of Mother Odilia's letter to St. Joseph written in German and dated 1874.

All the dear Sisters received Last Sacraments and pronounced their holy vows. It is a hard blow but it comes from our dear Bridegroom, Who in His great love sends it. We want to be resigned to His holy will. He knows what is best for us.

Dear Mother, ask all the children to pray much for us that we will persevere and, if God wills, come back home again.

We remain in the Sacred Hearts of Jesus and Mary,

Your obedient children,

The daily paper of a few days later, carried a similar tale of woe:

The epidemic has grown worse from day to day and up to the ninth of September 3,000 cases of yellow fever have been reported. One thousand two hundred deaths have occurred. Whole families are wiped out in one week; priests, sisters, and nurses are dying at their posts. The cry of the motherless is heard every hour, claiming the pity, the tears of the most hardened veterans.

Alas, fair Memphis, who will be left to tell the tale tomorrow? Hope, we have none! We despair of any relief, but we are nerved to the end.

We pray blessings upon the generous who have helped us in all the States. We pray for the safety of those who have come among us to nurse the sick, and to minister to the dying, and we ask that the names of the men and women who have laid down their lives for us be handed down forever as among the brightest and best of the earth.

In St. Louis, Mother Odilia received the news in horror. Over and over she begged, "Dear Father St. Joseph, guard our children and keep them safe." The knife twisted in her heart, for she was the one who had delivered these poor girls to death.

On September 6, at Sr. Margaret Mary's request, she allowed three more Sisters who had previously volunteered to go: Sisters Mechtildia, Bernardine, and Armella.

On September 10, she received the following telegram: "Send no more sisters! Sister Wilhelmine died today at eleven o'clock. Sisters Gertrude, Vincent and Stanislaus very low.

Father Aloysius"

111

Sister Vincent was indeed very ill. All day she prayed and sang in her delirium. Her sweet face was flushed and swollen. And chills which accompanied the fever made her shake in the bed piteously. Sister Armella never left her side at the Simms' home, wiping the black vomitus from her lips and softly praying in her ear, hoping that she understood but feeling almost certain that she did not, for she had been irrational since morning. The young nun could not understand Sister Armella for she was in the strange land of "in between" where one is separated from this world but has as yet not set foot in the next. In her delirium she prayed that her father would come back to the faith. Then in the same breath she would laugh wildly or hum a hymn. By nightfall her body was so worn out that Sister Armella was certain she would fall into a deep sleep and rest until morning. Then the vomiting began all over again, black and watery.

"Dear God," pleaded the tormented Sister-nurse, "hasn't this child suffered enough?"

The gentle Lover bending down, tenderly lifted His sacrificial spouse to His great heart. Just a little sigh escaped her purple lips as He gathered her up, like an expression of the ecstasy filling her noble soul as she beheld her Bridegroom.

Sister Vincent's father who had been trying to find his daughter again at last heard through Father Aloysius that she was nursing at the Simms' home.

Hurriedly he boarded a street car. He had not seen his daughter since she left Memphis three years ago against his wishes to enter the convent. Breathless, he arrived at the Simms' residence. But what a spectacle met his eyes! On a board on the floor lay his dear child, his rosy cheeked Bridget, now a yellow corpse. Her twisted black mouth, her parted lips, spoke more forcibly to his soul than any words she could ever have uttered. He had come just one hour too late!

A flood of tears burst from his eyes as he screamed in his sorrow. "She gave her earthly life that you might have eternal life," Sister Armella spoke to him quietly. Some hours later when he had regained his composure he and his wife bought the best coffin they could find and together accompanied their daughter's corpse to the cemetery. Immediately after the funeral a heavy-hearted John Hickey sought a priest to whom he made a general confession to gain at least peace of soul.

Next morning on awakening Mr. Hickey felt very weak, but he blamed it on his recent grief. Mrs. Hickey also experienced an enervating lassitude which was unusual to her healthy constitution. Could they have seen beyond the thin veil that envelops mortals, they would have caught sight of their Bridget in all her new beauty beckoning to them.

The fever lasted only a few days; both suffered intensely. One evening near sundown the Master came and together they joined their daughter in eternity.

It was Sister Margaret Mary writing again with trembling hands:

> Dear Mother,
> In the course of the last three days we have buried three of our dear Sisters. The fourth, Sister Gertrude's corpse, is still in the house. What can we do but pray, "Lord, Thy will be done, should it bring us pain or woe; Lord, may Thy will be done, though the reason we may not know?"
> All the Sisters had nice brown coffins with silver ornaments and also a nice wagon for burial.
> Doctor Nugent took care of us like a loving father and wanted to go to Sister Wilhelmine's funeral in spite of our warnings. The next day he was sick, and in less than one week we buried him. This was truly a great loss for us.
> We all ask pardon for the grief we have often caused you to have. Should it please the Lord that this be the last letter we write to you, we remain,
> Your obedient children in life and in death.

Needless to say, Mother Odilia's great heart was broken by this tragedy which struck her family. As she re-read the letter, the words bombarded her heart like pellets of lead tearing it to the very core. Then, through blinding tears, she wrote in return:

> My dear beloved children,
> Embracing you in spirit, I send you a hearty "God reward you!" What a prodigy of wisdom and love of God it is that

the Sacred Heart of Jesus had found and plucked such mature
fruit in the garden of His faithful servants, as yet so small and
young.

Saints we now have in heaven who are our guardian Angels,
our intercessors. The bridegroom called and they came forth.
Painful beyond measure it is for me, but when beheld in the
light of faith, what a grace! Therefore, my dear children, let
us persevere in perfect resignation to the holy Will of God.

If we can send you anything to alleviate and comfort you, tele-
graph at once. We shall do everything in our power to help
you.

A thousand greetings from all your companion Sisters who are
constantly praying and weeping for you, as is also
Your ever loving mother in the Sacred Heart,

Mother Mary Odilia.

Sad and fatiguing as these days were the Sisters experienced
real spiritual joys; they realized that many a soul found its way
to heaven through their ministration who would, perhaps, not
otherwise have done so.

Sister Mechtildis was sent to the home of a wealthy young
lady, Annette Watts, a victim of the plague. Miss Watts was very
ill and, as Sister entered, the girl reached out her hand to plead,
"Please help me."

Sister promised to do all she could for her, but when she
came back with the pan of water to begin the bath, the woman
noticed the rosary and crucifix. She sat half-way up in bed as if
to make sure she was not under a delusion. Then weakly falling
back on her soft pillow and gathering all her strength she said,
"I didn't know you were one of those . . . I asked for a nurse and
you are a Catholic and a Sister. I would not have you in my house
if I could get anyone else and as soon as the doctor can find some
other nurse to take care of me you will go immediately, do you
understand?" Then as she lay there panting in exhaustion, Sister
quietly bathed her tortured body and tried to make her comfortable.

Although Miss Watts maintained a sullen silence, her eyes
followed Sister's every moment, especially when, duties finished,
the weary nun paced up and down the thicky carpeted room saying

114

her rosary beads. Each time the doctor came to see his patient he commented on the splendid nursing care she was receiving.

Gradually Miss Watts' attitude changed as grace, through Mary's intercession, worked in her soul. How many of the rosaries Sister Mechtildis prayed as she sat through the long nights were offered for this woman God alone knows. Several days later Miss Watts called her to the side of the bed. Hesitantly she asked, "Would you teach me how to say those . . . those . . ."

"Rosary beads?" finished the astonished Sister. "Why I'd be glad to, but don't you think you should wait until you are stronger? You know the doctor does not want you to exert yourself. I'll continue to say them for you and, as soon as you gain a little more strength, I'll teach you. Then we can say them together."

But the troubled patient would not be put off. She was wealthy and pampered and would have her way in this as in all other matters. So, very slowly, Sister taught her new pupil. Two days later Miss Watts asked to be baptized and, as death was imminent, Sister pouring the waters of baptism over the head, gave to her the gift of salvation.

That night as the fever rose and she tossed about in her stupor, the suffering woman cried weird things. Every now and then she would be lucid enough to pray a halting Hail Mary. In her last clear moment with swollen tongue and blood oozing from her gums and nose she whispered "Tell my family I am so happy, so happy in the faith."

Sister Mechtildis held back the tears as she caught the blood in a pan. Then all was quiet—but just for a moment. Annette opened her eyes wide in surprise and looking up called, "Behold the Queen . . . behold the Queen of the Rosary!" Her eyes shut; the smile faded from her disfigured countenance. Sister knew that Annette Watts was already standing before the Queen who would escort her to the throne of the eternal King.

By September 13 the pestilence had reached its climax; hundreds of new cases were reported daily and the death rate was nearly one hundred every day. Sisters Margaret Mary and Bernardine were attacked by the fever on the morning of September 14 and Sister Armella later in the day. The last to come down with the disease was Sister Mechtildis. Before going to bed she put all their holy habits within reach and told the Sisters to put them on when they knew that death was approaching, for there would be no one to prepare them for burial. But God had work for them yet, and by October first they were well enough to nurse at their usual posts in the stricken city.

Canton, Mississippi, was also heavily hit by the plague and numerous were the letters which Mother Odilia received requesting aid.

Could she deepen the self-inflicted wound in her heart which now bled constantly? Could she send more of her Sisters to almost certain death? she wondered. But only until her eyes fell upon His crucified form; then there could be no hesitation for her.

On the feast of the Nativity of our Blessed Lady, Sisters Rose, Johanna, Petronilla, Josepha, and Francis arrived in Canton at the special request of the Right Reverend Bishop Elder, D.D. This made a total of thirteen Sisters that Mother Odilia had sent South from her small community of thirty-one members. She had now sacrificed more than one-third of the congregation in generosity and love.

The scenes which met the Sisters as they arrived in Canton were much like those experienced by the Sisters in Memphis. After first assisting at holy Mass, they set to work. Sister Petronilla was called to a house where there were twelve patients sick; Sister Francis went to care for a family of ten sick individuals. In one of her letters to Mother, she wrote . . . "Here I am surrounded by seven patients and three corpses."

Many were the comforting letters that the good Mother sorrowfully dispatched to her "exiled" children.

> My dear beloved good children,
> Yesterday evening our Holy Father, St. Joseph, brought us your dear letter and we were so happy to hear from you. Yes, my beloved children, the Sacred Heart of Jesus loves you much. Listen, my children, what St. Teresa says, "It is better to serve Christ than to receive Him." And now you are serving Him

on the cross. This is the only place where we can worthily serve Him.

Then she continued in a lighter strain to tell them of the happenings of St. Mary's convent and the orphanage. Yes, here the Sisters were carrying on their usual activities but a curtain of sadness hung over them. All the while their thoughts were with the absent members who were at the mercy of the scourge and at any moment might become its prey. Every day seemed to find her more weighted down with grief and sorrow. Many were the trips she made to the post office for news of her dear Sisters.

On this September afternoon when Postulant Sue returned with the letter from Canton, Mississippi, the good Mother thought her heart would break. With tears streaming down her sallow cheeks, she read:

> Canton, Mississippi
> Feast of the Stigmata of St. Francis
>
> Dear Reverend Mother,
> Our dear Lord has reaped in His garden and taken home the soul of His dearly beloved bride, our good Sister Johanna. Last night at 12:45 her death agony began. Reverend Father gave her general absolution and helped her pronounce her holy vows. In ten minutes she was gone. Sister's death was beautiful! I think the angels took her straight to heaven. Six hours before she died she sang a hymn to Blessed Mother in her delirium. She begged me to send greetings to you, dear Reverend Mother, and promised to remember you at the throne of God. She was buried this afternoon in a very poor coffin. Surely holy poverty!
>
> In Jesus' Sacred Heart,
> Sister M. Josepha

As Mother folded the letter, her small frame shook with convulsive sobbing. Five Sister martyrs and all between the ages of 21 and 27. "The cross is God's gift to His friends," the saintly Cure of Ars had said. Mother tried to remember these words now. Immediately she sought out her Comforter in the shadow of the sanctuary lamp.

It was hours later that Mother rose from her knees to go back to the little flock; not, however, until she had by her mute pleading won for the stricken "children" all the graces and strength they would need in the long days ahead. She was not thinking of herself, but like the windmill that must pump up the water to irrigate all the surrounding land and give life to the crops, she was drawing from this reservoir all the graces necessary for the spiritual life of her Sisters.

The plague did not abate and many a sorrowful letter continued to find its way to St. Joseph's Home. But the benevolent Mother's spiritually comforting letters which followed one another in rapid succession, brought great solace to the Sisters and helped dispel their loneliness. Frequently she sent packages containing wine, oranges, apples, bread, and other delectables, for very little could be purchased in the ravaged towns.

Writing to the Sisters on a collecting tour northwards into Wisconsin at this time, Mother gives a rare glimpse of the sorrow—and sickness too—that oppressed her.

> Dearly Beloved children,
> Today, I am some better, up and around. Grief and worry and bitter pain of soul for our dear good Sisters in the South has overwhelmed me. The heavenly Bridegroom came to get true pearls of Sisters. The loss of these members to the community only God and I can measure.

A sea of folded hands was lifted heavenward in petition. The whole nation was praying for the first frost. This was expected to put an end to the epidemic. Toward the end of October the relief came when the Memphis Board of Health declared the epidemic over. The number of yellow fever cases in Memphis from August 14 to November 4 was 17,600; of these 5,150 died. The Sisters of St. Mary cared for over 250 patients.

What a day of laughter and tears it was when the remaining eight of the thirteen Sisters who had gone south returned to the peaceful convent home in St. Louis. Holy Masses were offered for the deceased and Masses of thanksgiving for the safe return of survivors. The homecoming Sisters spent long hours before the Blessed Sacrament drinking deep of His Presence to slake their thirst for this luxury had been denied them the past months.

Festivities were planned and every effort was made to bring comfort and joy to the weary nuns. The Sisters who had remained in St. Louis outdid one another in preparing surprises for their companions in the way of extra rest and extra delicacies at the table, for surely the emaciated nuns needed them. But Mother Odilia outdid them all in her devotion; not so much by what she said but in her loving consideration of them which anticipated their every need. She could not do enough for them. Their dear Mother! She was not the plump, energetic woman they had left in August, but an exhausted little figure whose sunken eyes spoke of sorrow and holy resignation. With tears in her eyes she frequently referred to "our Community in heaven."

Father Faerber, their spiritual director, was in Europe when the Sisters returned from the South. He had gone abroad for his health early that year. But he sent a deeply spiritual and fatherly letter which Mother read to them next evening:

Paris, 1878

Venerable Mother and Sisters,
I arrived in Paris this afternoon from a visit to my dear sister. There were thirteen letters here waiting for me but, of course, I read yours first.

How deeply the wholly unexpected news which your letter contained grieved and pained me. I cannot express in words, much less can I transfer my feelings to paper. I can reveal them to God alone, and this I have already done. Immediately after reading your letter, I went to the Church of our Lady of Victories. There, kneeling before the Miraculous Altar of the Mother of God, I prayed for the good Sisters, who, true to their vocation, passed away in the Lord and for you, dear Mother.

The fact that a Congregation is blessed with a large number of Sisters who enjoy good health, is, in itself, no great honor; neither is it a proof of interior strength and stability. But that it has in its very beginning members who are faithful to their vocation and die for the same, this gives it as many foundation stones as there are oblations!

119

We now have powerful intercessors in heaven for our community; we stood in need of them and God has provided them for us. Deo Gratias!

My heartiest greetings to all the living and my fervent prayers for all the deceased members of the Community.

Yours in the Sacred Heart of Jesus,
Reverend William Faerber.

Although the religious and priests who nursed the yellow fever victims were gone from the unfortunate cities, they were not forgotten. Today in Calvary cemetery, Memphis, on a plot of ground surrounded by thick hedge and shaded by a large magnolia tree, there stands a monument to the memory of the twelve Sisters (four of them Sisters of St. Mary) and Brothers of various orders, who sacrificed their lives in the plague of 1878. This was erected by the Catholics of Memphis and St. Louis under the direction of the Knights of Columbus and was unveiled in 1928 by Sister Mechtildis, S.S.M., the only living survivor of the epidemic at that time.

The following year was a peacefully productive one for the Sisters. After the hard times they seemed to be given a respite to gather some strength. St. Joseph's Home became the most real source of joy to Mother Odilia, and she spent many happy hours playing with the children in the play yard, teaching them songs, listening to their chattering, answering their many questions.

Easter, as were all the big festivals of the year, was celebrated to the best of the Sisters' spiritual and financial means. After the High Mass, sung by the Sisters with the children, an egg hunt was held on the grounds.

September of 1879 found six more postulants standing before the altar eager to receive the holy habit of the Sisters of St. Mary. One was a young lady whom the Sisters had brought back with them on their return from Memphis. Truly the little congregation was advancing in "age and grace before God and man."

CHAPTER TEN

Let Her Works Praise
Her in the Gates

THE YEAR 1880 will forever be remembered by the Sisters of St. Mary for two reasons: an achievement and a loss.

A record breaking heat wave had swept the city of St. Louis and now in August devastation lay in its wake. The fields were seared to a yellow brown. Farmers were frantic as crops were ruined and whole herds of cattle died daily. Picking up the tattered umbrella, a very ineffectual protection against the scorching rays of the sun, Mother again went to the barn. She had made so many trips there in the last few days. How she pitied the poor animals, for the flat barns, exposed as they were to the merciless heat, gave them no comfort. A few panting white chickens teetered now on one foot and now on another, as if standing on hot coals. Mother walked past them into the barn. And there lay, just as she head feared, Brownie, the faithful horse, Milkyway, the cow, and two tame deer, stretched on the floor in a heap. Only yesterday she had found the two hogs, Fritz, the horse, and the other cow dead. Now all their livestock was wiped out. Mother wept! Like our holy Father, St. Francis, she felt sorry for the poor animals, but she felt more sorrow for the Sisters and the orphans. This would be a great loss for them.

"Dear Father Joseph," she prayed, "help us!" Then, standing in the middle of the shed, she whispered softly, "The Lord hath given, the Lord hath taken away. Blessed be the Name of the Lord!"

Mother's courage and holy resignation had long since become an essential part of her. Her trust embraced all things, from the lowest needs to her fondest spiritual aspirations, canonical status for her Community.

Coming back from the barn, Mother made her customary stop in the chapel. Leaving His Sacramental Presence some time later, she moved slowly now to her room and, strengthened by the spirit of encouragement, took up the worn pen. She would repeat still another time her plea for permission for herself and the members of her Community to pronounce the three holy vows of religion.

The Holy See is ever watchful over the many religious congregations of men and women established throughout the Catholic world. They must prove their worthiness by specific works of charity which are their secondary ends. The soul of a congregation, namely, the recognition and approbation of the Holy See, must be obtained. The approval of the Bishop of the diocese in which a congregation is established may be obtained, but the final and formal sanction of the Vicar of Christ must be had if that congregation is to enjoy the highest canonical status. This sanction is possible only after the congregation has proved its worthiness by years of work and by the religious life of its members.

The Sisters of St. Mary had now existed for eight years and had certainly proved their ability for work. Its members were actuated by a true spirit of charity to the extent of sacrificing their lives in behalf of suffering mankind. The life led by the Sisters had truly been one of a religious community. Up to this time they had lived according to the rule of the Third Order of St. Francis adapted to suit their specific secondary aim.

Mother Odilia realized the responsibility resting upon her; therefore it was her dearest wish to see the Community formally established.

There was evidence of this desire on the part of Mother as early as 1876 when in a letter to St. Joseph she wrote in part: "But now another favor I will ask of thee. We have that under way which we have delayed in fear; O dear St. Joseph, assist us; I leave to thee the choice of souls. Enlighten our ecclesiastical superiors. . . ."

Some difficulty was experienced in receiving the required permission. God was trying his favored souls. He would have them meet with delay, with seeming refusal. Yet Mother Odilia firmly believed that her request would be granted.

While the heartbreaking experience of the loss of her dear Sisters in the yellow fever plague had so weakened Mother physically, she seemed to increase marvelously spiritually. Purified by years of prayer, sacrifice, and holy abandonment to His holy will, she had only one desire — to unite herself and her Community to Him without reserve by the three holy vows of religion. She redoubled her prayers. She went to Mary!

A number of the Sisters, along with Mother Odilia, made a novena to our Lady of Perpetual Help at St. Alphonsus (Rock) Church, a distance of about three miles, which they walked each morning, hearing Mass, receiving Holy Communion, and invoking the aid of our Mother of Perpetual Help. Of course, it was only with great difficulty that Mother in her weakened condition could make this trip, but a superhuman strength seemed to drive her on to the goal she had envisaged these many years. As a drowning man seeing a life boat swims for it forgetting the angry waves on all sides, so Mother Odilia, seeing her life's ambition more of a possibility now than ever before, was insensible to the limitations of her body.

Kneeling before the miraculous picture, she prayed:

> Mother of Perpetual Help, with the greatest confidence, we come before thy sacred Picture, in order to invoke thine aid. Thou hast seen the wounds which Jesus has been pleased to receive for our sake; Thou hast seen the Blood of thy Son flowing for our salvation; thou knowest how thy Son desires to apply to us the fruits of his redemption. Behold, we cast ourselves at thy feet, and pray thee to obtain for our souls the graces we stand so much in need of. O Mary, most loving of all mothers, obtain for us from the Heart of Jesus, the source of all good, this grace, to receive Papal sanction and thereby

be permitted to make our Holy Profession. Mother of Perpetual Help, for the love thou bearest to Jesus, thy Son and our Redeemer, for the love of our souls, obtain for us this grace. Amen.

The rector, Father Meredith, C.SS.R., was most courteous to Mother and the Sisters, and urged them to persevere in their intention. At the close of the novena, the priest presented Mother Odilia with a framed copy of the miraculous picture. This picture has been carefully preserved and is venerated by the Congregation of the Sisters of St. Mary.

Again Mother's faith and trust in Mary was rewarded, for shortly after the novena ended they received from Pope Leo XIII the desired permission to pronounce their Holy Vows. A foretaste of the joys of heaven flooded the little community when Mother announced the good news.

On September 27, in accordance with Mother's orders, a retreat was begun in preparation for the happy event. On the morning of October 4, Feast of St. Francis of Assisi, in the chapel of the Motherhouse at St. Joseph's Home, Very Reverend Vincent Halbfass, O.F.M., Provincial of the Franciscan Fathers, celebrated Mass at seven o'clock, during which the Sisters received Holy Communion. At eight o'clock, Father Faerber sang the High Mass at the conclusion of which the Very Reverend Monsignor Henry Muehlsiepen received the vows of Mother Mary Odilia and Sisters Mary Magdalene, Elizabeth, Francis, Odilia, Teresa, Clara, Agnes, Rose, Bernardine, Antonia, Salesia, Mechtildis, Seraphia, Petronilla, Cecilia, and Margaret Mary. The Bridegroom had come to these seventeen patient, valiant brides.

With a heart bursting with love and gratitude, Mother Odilia and each Sister in turn repeated the formula:

I, ... , vow and promise to Almighty God, to the Blessed Mary, ever Virgin, and to our Holy Father Francis to live in obedience, poverty, and chastity according to the Rule given by His Holiness Leo X for the Members of the Third Order of St. Francis living in community and according to the Constitutions of our Congregation of the Sisters of St. Mary.

Now they were truly His! They had formally promised to live in servitude out of love to Jesus Christ.

Busano in his "Expositio Regulae," pays the following tribute to the excellence of the religious profession:

> Religious profession is a most perfect sacrifice of oneself, because the one making it renounces all earthly goods by the vow of poverty, the licit joys of family life by the vow of chastity, and self determination by the vow of obedience; and thus, according to the common teaching, she performs an act so great and so heroic that it can be compared to martyrdom; for even though the professed religious does not die a violent death by the sword, nevertheless, because of the continual denial of her lower passions and the pressing yoke of religious austerity, she undergoes a sort of mystical death. For this reason, it is the common opinion of theologians that the effect of religious professions is a remission of all punishment due to sins, not indeed in virtue of profession itself, because it is not a sacrament, but because of its atoning value which is a meet satisfaction for all the debt due to sin.

Fervently Mother Mary Odilia kissed her vow formula. It was a new contract she had entered into symbolic of the triple cord which now bound her irrevocably to her Spouse. Oh, how happy she was! Did this not more than compensate for all the years of hardship and suffering? Bowing her head she fervently prayed: "Dear Jesus, tighten every day, more and more these cords which unite us to Thee and never permit that any one of us should seek to loose herself from them. May the members of this Community ever be a joy and comfort to Thee by their good and holy lives; may they live and die as faithful spouses of their crucified Love."

The privileges which this day were brought to the Sisters of Saint Mary were attributed to the special intercession of our Mother of Perpetual Help. Devotion to the Mother of God under this title, has been a very intimate and sacred one in the Congregation since that time.

After the day of their holy Profession, the Sisters returned to their various works with renewed spiritual vigor. Everything they did now had an added luster; each act became an act of the virtue of religion. Joy and peace reigned in the little community and the very walls echoed the Sisters' prayer: "Behold, what I have coveted I see already; what I hoped, I hold even now; to Him I am joined in heaven whom, I while placed on earth, have loved with all my heart."

Later that week Sister Theresa sitting in the recreation room with her companions whispered: "Doesn't Mother look pale to-night?"

"Yes, I've been thinking that, too," returned Sister Rose.

"But did you notice also that she eats so little these days?" put in Sister Antonia.

"She must be ill," Sister Theresa concluded.

"I know she is ill," chimed in Sister Francis. "I've been watching her closely myself."

"Oh, Mother has been sick for a long time now, but she is trying to conceal it," interposed the wise Sister Margaret Mary. "In fact, she has not been herself since we went South. That was an awful blow for her!"

So by the "grapevine" word was passed on that Mother was ill. And as we all must admit, there are times when these "grapevine" messages contain a large percentage of truth. Mother Odilia was completely oblivious of this conversation of which she was the topic. With trembling fingers, she was sewing huge patches on the knees of a pair of little boys' overalls while forcing herself to be gay and join in the fun.

Next day found her in the play room with the little ones. This was her favorite haunt. But she was not joining in their rowdy games as usual. Today she was helping the smaller group clustered around the oval table with their drawing. Franklin and Carol could dream up the most bizarre creatures and the table was literally cluttered with the products of their four year old imaginations. Along the outside of the table stood Lucy's dainty clay and saucer "Fit for a queen," complimented Mother. And she was rewarded by a queenly hug from the diminutive Lucy. Then it

126

was Mother Odilia's turn and she fashioned a little Sister of St. Mary from the soft clay, which made the whole roomful of children squeal with delight.

But she could not stay long in the noisy playroom and once back in her own room she pressed her hot cheeks against the cool ledge of the window. She would rest awhile before going down to dinner. That was all Mother remembered.

When she awoke, she was in bed and Doctor Charles Garcia was bending over her. It was Sunday, October tenth. Mother made an effort to speak but Doctor interrupted her, "Save your strength, Mother. You must stay in bed and, please, do try to eat. We'll have you up and feeling your old self again before you know it." Mother smiled weakly at her old friend.

Once downstairs and out of Mother's hearing, Doctor Garcia confided to Sister Rose, Mother's nurse, "Her condition is serious— the typhoid fever may be back. I'm going to have Doctor Gregory and two other doctors come over to see her this evening. Prepare her for this so she won't be alarmed. Keep her in bed and try to get her to take some nourishment. I'll have the druggest bring a medication over for her pain." Then shaking his head sadly, he continued, "You know, Sister, these last years have been very hard on Mother. She began failing when the Sisters went South to nurse the yellow fever victims. I noticed that myself; she hasn't been the same since."

"Yes," whispered Sister Rose half to herself. "Mother was with us all the while in spirit and each time the death of one of the Sisters was reported to her, a little more of her own life's blood was drained from her body."

Sister Rose saw the doctor to the door. Then wiping the tears from her eyes, she hastily went back to the sick room. Mother did not see her come in. Her eyes were closed but her lips moved slowly as our Lady's beads slipped through her thin fingers.

Sitser Rose prepared the most tempting food, but it was almost impossible for Mother to take any food at all.

That afternoon the dying Mother asked that the orphans be brought to see her. Sister Rose feared to grant the request, knowing how difficult it would be to keep them quiet. But Doctor Garcia readily granted the permission.

"We cannot deny her anything now," he said simply, and Sister guessed what he meant. So the next day, with Mother propped up in bed, the little ones were brought in small groups to visit her. For the most of them, she was the only earthly Mother they had ever known. Although too weak to speak, she had for each a smile and a blessing. But when Lucy came, almost in the last group, clutching the clay nun which she put in bed with Mother, the tears which had been so bravely held back, streamed down her cheeks and it was Lucy who, in her childlike way, took the edge of the coverlet and wiped them away.

"They should never have been permitted to come," scolded Sister Francis after the last child had left. "Look how it has weakened Mother."

"But Doctor Garcia wanted Mother's wish to be granted," defended the patient Sister Rose.

Each of the next three days found Mother a little weaker and, when peritonitis set in, all hope for her recovery was given up. But she was not alarmed. "My work is accomplished," she announced. "My family has grown up. I am tired."

To the priest who administered Extreme Unction to her she remarked, "One must always be resigned to God's will, especially when His will is one's death. One might plead for recovery, but only on condition that God wills it."

All the Sisters were present. Mother frequently made ejaculations to the Sacred Heart of Jesus and exhorted the Sisters in a feeble voice ever to be devoted to this great Heart, their first Love. The smoky oil lamp cast weird shadows of the kneeling nuns on the pale walls.

Sadness descended like a pall not only on St. Joseph's Home but over the other two houses as well. All the time the Sisters could spare from duty was spent before the tabernacle in petition for their Mother. But, like Mother, they too prayed, "Not as we will, but as Thou willest."

At any hour of the day the orphans could be seen in the chapel, their heads barely visible above the high pews, praying for their

Mother. Chubby hands joined in petition, eyes closed tightly, and lips moving audibly. What they were saying God alone knows. But we may be sure that in their simplicity they begged Him to let their Mother get well. And He bending down to their littleness whispered, "If I do take your Mother, dear, I will give you My Mother. You will never really be an orphan as long as you live, for My own Mother, the best, will care for you."

Saturday found Mother much weaker and now it was Sunday, October 17, just 13 days after she had pronounced her Holy Vows. The goodness of God had let her live just long enough to realize her life's ambition and to enhance her glory for all eternity! How very near her "dear Father, St. Joseph," was at this hour.

At three o'clock her death agony began. Father Faerber, three Franciscan priests and the Sisters recited the prayers for the dying.

> When in death my limbs are failing
> Let Thy Mother's prayer prevailing
> Lift me, Jesus, to Thy throne.

They could see she was being slowly lifted to His throne.

> To my parting soul be given
> Entrance through the gate of heaven
> There confess me for Thy own. (Stabat Mater)

At four o'clock the Christ of the Divine Heart came for His humble servant.

Mother Mary Odilia's death occurring as it did on the feast of St. Margaret Mary, confidante of the Sacred Heart, coincided with the same day, fourteen years before, on which the Community of the Sister Servants of the Divine Heart of Jesus was organized by her in Paris.

Ironically, perhaps fortuitively, the death of Mother Mary Odilia, who had devoted so many years to administering to the victims of smallpox, also coincided with the introduction by Louis Pasteur of the successful vaccine against smallpox and initiated scientific control of the monster disease.

129

At the time of her death Mother Odilia was in the fifty-eighth year of her life, the twenty-sixth year of her religious life, and the eighth year of her life in America.

Her body was taken to St. Mary's convent where it lay in state until the following Tuesday morning. The funeral took place from St. Mary's Church, Tuesday, October 19, 1880, at nine o'clock in the morning. Persons of every age and station came to pay a last tribute to the Venerable Mother, for truly she was mother, not only to the sick poor of St. Louis, but to those throughout the Midwest and South as well. After Mass, the funeral procession consisting of Reverend Father Faerber, the entire Community of Sisters and the orphans from St. Joseph's Home, wended its sorrowful way to Calvary cemetery. There they left that little body in which had resided so great and magnanimous soul.

As they were going back to their convent homes that morning a piercing sadness filled the heart of each Sister such as the Mother of God must have felt when, after placing her broken Son in the tomb, she sorrowfully turned to go back to the city. But just as deep beneath the ocean of Mary's sorrow, there ran a tranquil stream of peace which was the assurance of His resurrection, so beneath the sorrow in each Sister's heart there flowed the comforting conviction that Mother Odilia was not really dead. Her spirit would continue to live and grow in the Sisters of Saint Mary. She herself would still be governing them only now from a higher vantage point.

Thus ended a life of failure after failure which was in the end crowned with events that turned it into one of America's great success stories. By seeking to imitate her Divine Redeemer through her work as nurse and nun, she grew in faith, determination and discipline. Her monumental achievements in the business of charity brought down upon her daughters a fertility of a sort valued highly in the realm of the spirit.

PRAYER

Most Sacred Heart of Jesus, Who hast promised to pour out abundant benedictions on all the undertakings of those who practice devotion to Thy Divine Heart be mindful of the merits and prayers of Thy handmaid, our Venerable Foundress, Mother Mary Odilia, who during her life on earth heroically overcame all difficulties and hardships through Thy most powerful aid.

Assured that our Mother is also pleading our petition, we are confident that you will hear our prayers inasmuch as it is conductive to Thy greater glory and our eternal salvation.